PAUL'S
EPISTLE TO THE
ROMANS

E. F. SCOTT, D.D.

PAUL'S EPISTLE TO THE ROMANS

GREENWOOD PRESS, PUBLISHERS
WESTPORT, CONNECTICUT

Library of Congress Cataloging in Publication Data

Scott, Ernest Findlay, 1868-1954.
  Paul's epistle to the Romans.

  Reprint of the 1947 ed. published by S.C.M. Press,
London.
  Includes index.
  1. Bible. N.T. Romans--Commentaries. I. Title.
BS2665.S37 1979   227'.1'06   79-4204
ISBN 0-313-20800-X

First published March 1947 by the Student Christian Movement
Press, 56 Bloomsbury St., London W.C.1

Reprinted with the permission of SCM Press Ltd.

Reprinted in 1979 by Greenwood Press, Inc.
51 Riverside Avenue, Westport, CT 06880

Printed in the United States of America

10 9 8 7 6 5 4 3 2 1

CONTENTS

PREFACE

THERE is no lack of excellent commentaries on the Epistle to the Romans. Perhaps it has suffered from too much exposition, and many people have grown afraid of a work which cannot be understood without such exhaustive study. They assume that it is abstruse and difficult, and must be left to professional scholars. This was certainly not the design of Paul. He wrote a letter, addressed to a miscellaneous group of Christians. He sought to make clear to them the primary truths of their religion, and so inspire them with faith and ardour and self-devotion. The theological argument is nothing but a means to this practical end which he had in view. It is the aim of the present book to fix attention, not so much on the incidental puzzles of the Epistle, as on its main intention. What are the principles of Christianity as Paul here presents them? How does he apply them to the needs of his time? How can we give effect to them in our world to-day, which is so different from that of Paul and yet, in many respects, so like it? The Epistle to the Romans, for all its wrappings of ancient thought and language, is essentially a modern book, and only when we so read it can we apprehend its true message.

E. F. SCOTT

I

THE ORIGIN AND PURPOSE
OF THE EPISTLE

THE Epistle to the Romans is the weightiest and most elaborate of Paul's writings, and is therefore placed before the others in our New Testament. This arrangement has in some ways been unfortunate. Many readers are apt to form their whole impression of Paul's teaching from this opening letter, which they find obscure and difficult, and wholly concerned with matters of doctrine. They infer that while he was doubtless a profound thinker Paul was cold and intellectual, more concerned with the problems of Christianity than with its vital message. In the letters which follow they would come to know him as an intensely human personality, tender, impulsive, generous, passionately loyal to his friends and to Christ his Master; but they stop short with his first Epistle, and in Paul the theologian they lose sight entirely of Paul the man.

The Roman Epistle itself cannot be rightly understood when it is isolated from the others. To all appearance it is a work of abstract reflection. There is little to indicate that the writer had any end in view but to examine and justify the accepted Christian beliefs. He treats them almost like mathematical propositions, intent only on proving, by rules of logic, that they are true. Much of the modern criticism of Romans would seem to rest on this assumption, and since the reasoning of Paul is sometimes, to our minds, unconvincing, it is shown that he has failed in his object and that his Epistle may now be thrown aside. But the man who wrote it was also the author of the Corinthian letters and of Galatians and Philippians. In these Epistles also Paul argues about his faith, but his main purpose is to kindle in others that fire of devotion which burns in his own heart. They may think what they will of his opinions, but he wishes them to feel, as he does, that the gospel is God's own message to men and brings with it a new life. This, we may be sure, is also his purpose in the Epistle to Romans. Behind the argument there is the living conviction of a man whom Christ had saved and who believed that He would likewise save the world.

The Epistle, therefore, cannot be understood apart from the man. Scholars have enquired diligently in recent years into the various sources from which Paul may have derived some of his ideas, and there can be no question that he was largely indebted to thinkers before him. But in the last resort the Epistle is a personal document. Paul expresses a faith which was intimately his own. He draws on his actual experiences, and tests every statement by what he has known and felt himself. The Epistle begins with a brief account of who he was and how he had been called to his Apostolic work, and in this knowledge of the writer we must find the key to everything in the letter which follows.

It so happens that this letter can be fitted more accurately than any of the others into the framework of Paul's career. Romans is in many ways the most difficult of the Epistles, but at least the approaches to it are clear of the usual obstacles. We know definitely when it was written and where, and in a general sense for what purpose. Paul had finished his work at Ephesus and was re-visiting Corinth, in fulfilment of a long-standing promise. The three years through which he had lately passed had been the most trying he had yet known. Not only had his labours grown heavier, but he had been assailed on every side by enemies. Hostile teachers from Jerusalem had followed in his track, and had tried to pervert his churches to a Jewish type of Christianity. Among his Gentile converts there were many who sought to dissolve the new religion in a modified Paganism. The Roman authorities who had hitherto been friendly were now suspicious of the Christian movement, and in Ephesus he had been mobbed and ill-treated as a dangerous agitator, and at one time had lain under sentence of death. Besides all this, his beloved church at Corinth had for some reason turned against him. The quarrel had continued bitterly for a long time, and he had finally been compelled to write a stern letter in the nature of an ultimatum. After waiting anxiously to learn the effect of this last appeal he made his way towards Corinth, and met his messenger returning with good news. The visit he had dreaded was now one of joy and reconciliation.

At Corinth he remained for some months, expecting the delegates from the Gentile churches who were to accompany him to Jerusalem. For several years he had been occupied with the collection of a sum of money for the relief of Christians in Palestine who had fallen into poverty. This was to be his peace-offering to the mother-church which had become estranged from him, and was also to serve as a visible proof that the churches of Christ, however divided, were one in spirit and eager to help each other. The money was now gathered in, and to make the gift more impressive he had arranged that every church should send its own spokesman to share in the presentation. The party was now assembling and would sail when the sea was open. It was in these winter months, probably A.D. 57-58, that he wrote the Epistle to the Romans.

It is necessary to keep these facts in mind in order to explain some features of this Epistle which distinguish it from all the others. Paul was now enjoying almost the first interval of peace which had fallen to him since his missionary work began. His mood was one of ease and tranquillity after a long period of strain, and it is reflected in his letter. He writes at leisure and can develop his thought in orderly sequence and take pains with his language. He reasons calmly with those who differ from him, and refrains from those outbursts of anger into which he is sometimes hurried in his other letters. If it had been written more hastily, under a strong excitement, the Epistle might have been more interesting, but it reveals Paul to us in his more habitual frame of mind. He must have composed this letter with more pleasure than any of the others. For the time being he was free from outward anxieties, and could forget himself wholly in the great ideas which crowded in upon him.

His letter is addressed to the church at Rome, which as yet he had never visited. How this church had come into existence is one of the riddles of Christian history. It was associated by later tradition with the name of Peter, but if Peter was ever in Rome, which is by no means certain, he must have arrived when the Roman church was already flourishing. In Galatians and 2 Corinthians, which were written shortly before Romans, Paul seems to take for granted that Peter was still one of the leaders of the church in Palestine. He writes to the Roman church as to one that was now firmly established and had won a place among the foremost of Christian communities. For a long time, he says, he had been hearing about it, and had resolved on several occasions to see it for himself, but had hitherto been prevented. He can speak of it in this manner less than thirty years after the Crucifixion, and we can thus infer that almost at the beginning Christianity had found its way to Rome. Perhaps it had come through chance travellers who were constantly arriving in the great city which was the centre of everything. Or perhaps a church had been founded in Rome by followers of Stephen after their expulsion from Jerusalem. Most of them, like Stephen himself, were Jews of the Dispersion, and when Palestine was closed to them they returned to the various Gentile cities from which they had come. Among them there were certain to be a number from Rome, and when they settled again in their former surroundings they would form a Christian community. If this was the origin of the Roman church, as appears more than likely, we can well understand that from the first it would be liberally minded. Stephen had protested against the narrowing and externalizing of religion. He had been martyred because he had questioned the sanctity of the Temple, and perhaps of the Law itself. A church formed by his disciples would be favourably disposed towards

Paul's free gospel, and he assumes throughout his Epistle that his readers will be in sympathy with him. We can gather from his allusions that while some of them were strict Jews the majority were either Gentiles or shared in the Gentile point of view. The community at Rome may not yet have formally discarded the Law, but it treated the legal demands as subordinate, and laid all the emphasis on faith in Christ.

It is unfortunate that so little is known to us of the Roman church at this time, for in writing his Epistle Paul doubtless keeps his audience before his mind. Sometimes it has been maintained that Romans is not properly a letter, but is rather a discourse or a theological essay thrown into epistolary form. Paul, however, never wrote aimlessly in this fashion. " I am not," he declares in 1 Corinthians, " as one who beateth the air." He needed to have definite people in his mind's eye, and gave all that he said an application to their particular needs. To be sure he had never been in Rome, and those whom he addressed were still strangers to him; but the Christian sect was a small one, and its scattered communities were closely in touch with one another. It was an age of travel, and wherever he went Paul would meet with someone who had lately been at Rome. His dearest friends, Aquila and Priscilla, with whom he had lodged for several years, belonged to Rome, and would still have connections there. It would indeed have been a sheer impertinence on the part of Paul to write this letter if he was quite ignorant of the people he wrote to, and had never troubled to inform himself. We may be sure that he knew much about them, and that he makes constant use of his knowledge.

Some of the difficulties we meet with in the Epistle are due to nothing else than our want of acquaintance with the Roman church and the conditions which prevailed in it. No letter can be properly understood by a stranger. There are sure to be hints and references in it which have no meaning except to the person or the circle for whom it is intended. If we are puzzled by a number of things in Romans we must remember that it was not written for us but for a company

B

of Christians in first-century Rome. They would recognize the point of much in the argument which to us appears dull or irrelevant. The complaint is often made that Paul does not write a letter but a treatise, and a highly abstruse one. He turns the Christian message into a labyrinth of doctrine, which often has little to do with actual human experience. The first readers, we can hardly doubt, felt very differently. Passages in the Epistle which now seem of no importance may have touched their dearest interests. Ideas which to our minds are purely academic may have given them just the practical guidance which they needed most. This Epistle to Romans is beset with many difficulties, but the chief one is that it is an Epistle, a personal letter to which only the writer and his immediate readers held the clue.

One thing is made abundantly clear by Paul himself. He writes from Corinth to the church at Rome to prepare the way for his coming visit. He tells that he will not be able to make it for some time, for he has still to complete the important business which he has on hand. He has collected money in aid of the church at Jerusalem, and must see it safely delivered in that distant city; only then will he be free to make his journey to Rome, which is to be his starting-point for a new mission to the west. Ever since he began his missionary work he had kept a great plan before him—to proclaim the gospel to the whole Gentile world. This plan was not so extravagant as it seems to us now, when we think of vast regions still ignorant of Christianity after the labour of countless missionaries during two thousand years. How could one man expect in his own lifetime to evangelize the whole world? We must remember, however, that the world, for Paul, meant only the Roman empire, and he never intended to visit every corner of the empire and make his voice heard by everybody. He believed that the gospel possessed an inherent life, in virtue of which it would diffuse itself when it was once planted. It would be enough, therefore, to found small churches in two or three of the chief cities of the thirty provinces into which the empire was divided. From these centres the light would radiate out into the surrounding country and the beacon on one height would cause others to be kindled. Paul had decided, also, that he would not go where the gospel had been preached already, and was thus able to leave out of his itinerary such lands as Egypt and the regions east of Palestine. With these restrictions his plan was not so fantastic. Already, after six or seven years' labour, he had covered the eastern provinces, and if he had been allowed another equal period of active work he might have carried out his scheme. As he rested at Corinth he was turning his mind to the west. This was henceforth to be his field, and the west could only be approached through Rome. All the roads branched off from the great capital. Any movement that was to count for anything had to find its impulse and support in the city to which all western lands looked with veneration. Paul was well aware that his new mission would have little chance of success unless he could make sure that the church in Rome was behind him.

He found himself, however, in a difficulty. The resolve he had made never to go where other teachers had been before him was generally known, and Rome not only possessed the gospel but was the seat of a great church, proud of its status and independence. The Roman Christians might well regard his visit as an intrusion, and see in it some design to set up a rival community, or to change their beliefs and practices. He feels it necessary to assure them by this previous letter that he is not coming as an interloper, and that his object is not to reform or criticize but simply to ensure their help in advancing the common cause.

He writes, then, to introduce himself to the church at Rome, and for this purpose a short, friendly letter would have been sufficient, and no one could have done it better than the man who wrote the Epistle to Philemon. Moreover, if he had only wished to inform them that he was coming he would not have written so long in advance. The Romans would receive his letter while he was still in the early stages of his journey to Jerusalem, and he could not expect to be with

them for many months to come. In this long interval they
might easily forget all about him, or events might happen, as
in fact they did, which would completely change his plans.
Why was it that when his visit was still in an uncertain
future he chose to write this long Epistle, which is not so
much a personal letter as a reasoned exposition of the main
principles of the Christian faith?

According to one view, which had many advocates in the
last century, he wished to put his teaching on record for all
time to come. He knew that his life was in danger and his
work as good as finished. While there was still time he drew
up this full and explicit statement of how he understood the
Christian message. He meant it to be his religious will and
testament, and to whom could he better entrust it than to
the Roman church, which was destined, as he clearly saw, to
be first among all the churches? He therefore made his
projected visit the excuse for writing this manifesto and sending it to the premier church for safe keeping. There may
be some truth in this theory, but it lies open to several grave
objections. For one thing, the Epistle by no means contains
the whole of Paul's teaching. It deals for the most part with
a single doctrine, and does not expound it in all its aspects.
If other writings of Paul had not been preserved, much that
is essential in his thought would be unknown to us. Again,
the Epistle bears all the marks of a real letter. It is not meant
for future times or for the church at large, but for Roman
Christians at one particular time. It takes account of their
special difficulties and is full of allusions which would hardly
be intelligible to other readers. It cannot be merely a tract
or pamphlet in disguise. Once more, Paul did not write it
with the thought in his mind that his work was finished and
that he must now gather up his message in one final utterance.
On the contrary he felt that he was only in mid-career. All
that he had done hitherto was by way of preparation. He
had proclaimed the gospel in the eastern lands, where he was
most at home; now he was to launch out into that great
western world which as yet he only knew by rumour. This

would be the real test of his enterprise. If he could win those aliens to the faith in Christ he would prove conclusively that it was meant for all mankind.

He wrote this Epistle, therefore, with other motives than to put his teaching on record, and so preserve it for future times. His aims were much more definite and practical, and it is not hard to discover what they were. He was aware, for one thing, that he was regarded by a large section of the church with grave suspicion. For years past the Jewish party at Jerusalem had set itself to countermine his work. Its emissaries had followed him wherever he went, persuading his converts that in detaching the gospel from the Law he had taught a false Christianity. As controversialists are wont to do they had maligned his personal character, attributing to him all manner of base and sinister motives. There could be little doubt that as soon as his plans were known these men would proceed to Rome, and perhaps some of them were there already. It was necessary that he should be beforehand with them, and offer the Romans a true statement of what he believed, with special reference to points in his teaching which had been called in question. This is what he does in the Epistle. He seeks to remove the ignorant prejudices which had been raised against him, and defends his positions where they were most likely to be assailed.

This motive, however, is a secondary one, and along with it we can discern another, which weighed infinitely more with Paul than any desire to clear his own reputation. He was planning a mission to remote countries, to Spain and Gaul and perhaps to Britain. In these half-barbarous people the Roman Christians would take little interest. Jews and Greeks and the races of Asia Minor were within their own circle, and they could understand the need of imparting to them their knowledge of the Christian salvation. Paul was bent, however, on carrying his message to countries outside the pale. He knew that his enterprise would be hopeless without the co-operation of the Roman church. His chief purpose in going to Rome was to make sure of this assistance, and his visit would be fruitless if he could not awaken the Roman church to a sense of man's universal need, and of the power of Christianity to answer it. In almost every verse of the Epistle there is some word that denotes totality. All have sinned; all will be judged; between race and race there is no difference; in Christ all will be made alive; He lives for ever and the life He gives is eternal. The whole Epistle is written around the theme that men have fundamentally the same nature, and the gospel has the same value for all mankind. Jews and Greeks and barbarians have all erred alike; the deliverance won by Christ is open to all, and all are capable of that act of faith by which alone they can obtain it. From this it follows that those who have received the gospel have no right to keep it to themselves. It belongs by its very nature to all human beings and must be freely offered to all. In the course of his Epistle Paul seems often to wander, but he never fails to come back to this idea of the universality of the gospel. Men must all share it with their fellow-men, since it is God's answer to the central human need.

Here, then, we must look for the inner purpose of the Epistle. Paul had planned a visit to Rome, and writes to introduce himself to the Roman Christians. He has often thought of them, and looks forward to meeting them, and is anxious to remove all misunderstandings which might interfere with his welcome. Yet he is not coming as a mere friendly visitor. He intends that Rome should be his point of departure for that mission to the unknown west which will put the crown on all his previous labours. If he is to carry it out successfully he must have the Roman Christians heartily on his side, and with this end in view he tries to bring home to them the unlimited scope of the gospel and the responsibility it lays on them. The letter in which he announces his coming thus takes the form of a profound enquiry into the meaning of the Christian religion. We speak of Romans as a theological Epistle, but the theology is all subordinate to the practical purpose which Paul has in mind. " I am not ashamed of the gospel of Christ, for it is the power of God unto salvation to every one that believeth." This is Paul's own statement of his motive in writing to the Romans, and he speaks of two things which he wishes to impress on them. On the one hand, the gospel is no mere interesting speculation but an active power which is capable of transforming the world. On the other hand, it is intended for everyone. It needs to be noted that the emphasis in the familiar verse is on the concluding words. The gospel provides what all men are seeking for, and all are capable of the faith which can respond to it.

It is necessary to keep in mind that Paul writes with a practical purpose, for we are constantly told that in our time, when the world is faced with so many terrible realities, there is no place for the religious theorizing of the Epistle to Romans. This common idea of Paul as a mere spinner of doctrines which have no bearing on the actualities of life is indeed a strange one. He might truly say to our present-day apostles of a practical gospel as he said to those of his own time, " I laboured more abundantly than you all." He wrote this letter to the Romans in a brief interval of rest between two periods of incessant toil. He was on the road to Palestine with a large sum of money which he had collected by his own exertions for the relief of the unemployed. If ever there was a man whose Christianity was practical it was the Apostle Paul, and to hold him up as a theorist, who turned the gospel of action into a metaphysic, is nothing else than ridiculous. The Epistle to Romans is written for the express purpose of supplying the energy which would push forward a great work. Paul was entering on the most arduous of all his labours. He had determined to win new nations for the cause of Christ, and could do nothing without helpers. He desires the Roman Christians so to understand the gospel that they will share his own faith and courage, and work along with him for the welfare of their fellow-men. His Epistle, when we look below the surface, is not an exposition of doctrine but an inspiring call to Christian action. This was what it meant to its first readers, and it is from this point of view that we should read it still.

The Epistle falls into three main sections, which may seem at first sight to be quite unconnected with each other. In the main section (chapters i-viii) Paul offers his interpretation of the gospel as the message of God's free gift to men, to be received by faith. In the second section (ix-xi) he deals with the specific question of the destiny of Israel, whom God had chosen as His people and had apparently rejected. The third section (xiii-xv. 12) is of a purely practical character, with special reference to conditions at Rome. Paul tells his readers how they should order their individual lives, how they should perform their duties as citizens, how they should promote the welfare and harmony of the church. In the remainder of the fifteenth chapter he speaks of his own circumstances and plans, and begs the Roman Christians to remember him in their prayers. The sixteenth chapter consists mainly of salutations and is probably to be regarded as a separate letter which has been accidentally attached to the Roman Epistle. Phoebe, a deaconess of Cenchreae, the port of Corinth, is travelling to another city, apparently Ephesus, and Paul furnishes her with a short note of introduction, and takes this occasion of sending his greetings to the many friends who were still fresh in his remembrance. On many grounds, as we shall see later, this account of the closing chapter is almost certainly the right one.

The Epistle thus appears to break into several independent parts, and many attempts have been made to find a connection between them. Since this is difficult some scholars have maintained that the Epistle as we have it is a compilation. Several letters of Paul have been stitched together in a patchwork under the general heading of the Epistle to the Romans. A theory of this kind is unnecessary, for we have to deal not with a formal treatise but with a letter, and in a letter you do not expect a logical sequence. Paul himself in his other Epistles often passes without warning from one subject to another, as we all are wont to do when writing to our friends.

We need also to bear in mind that the first readers would see connections which are now obscure. For us the chapters on the destiny of Israel have little to do with the main argument that salvation must be by faith, but the Roman Christians, for whom the letter was intended, may have felt, for some reason, that the two themes went together. The church in Rome was made up of both Jews and Gentiles, and even the most vital beliefs could not be separated from party issues. In our ignorance of the conditions for which he wrote we cannot charge Paul with incoherence because we cannot now trace the links of his thought. It was he, after all, who wrote the letter, and presumably he knew better than we can do how he should frame it for the audience he had in view.

In one sense, however, the Epistle is all of a piece, even though its several parts seem to be unconnected. It has been assumed too generally that Paul's whole purpose in Romans was to work out an argument. When his logic halts, or when he shifts from one line of reasoning to another, he is supposed to have missed his way. A mathematician once complained of *Paradise Lost* that it did not prove anything, and much of the criticism of Romans has been of the same order. The poet was not trying to work out a demonstration, neither was the Apostle. They must both be judged by the manner in which they accomplished what they had set themselves to do. The aim of Paul was to impress on his readers the essential meaning of the gospel, so that they might believe in it and impart it to others. He would not have been much disturbed if it had been pointed out to him that his argument was loose and disjointed. He could have shown that never for a moment had he lost hold of his central idea that the gospel is a divine power, through which we have redemption and newness of life. In so far as it makes real to us the nature of the Christian message the Epistle is one with itself from beginning to end.

The closing chapter, while it is undoubtedly the work of Paul, is most probably to be taken as a separate letter, and it has been held by some scholars that the fifteenth chapter is

likewise an addition. In a number of ancient manuscripts the
Epistle closes with xiv. 23, followed by the doxology which
now stands at the end of the sixteenth chapter. How this
confusion arose it is difficult to see, for the fifteenth chapter
is the natural continuation of the one before, and in every
sentence it bears the hall-mark of Paul's style and thought.
It cannot be doubted, however, in face of the manuscript
evidence, that copies of the Epistle were in circulation at an
early time in which the fifteenth chapter was wanting. The
explanation may be that Romans was accepted almost from
the first as the authoritative statement of the Christian faith,
and was used as a text-book of religious instruction. For this
purpose an abridgment was felt to be desirable, and the part
which could most easily be dispensed with was that which
contained no doctrine, but consisted wholly of personal
notices, meant only for the first readers. This section was
left out, and since the Epistle thus ended very abruptly a
doxology was added. Perhaps it is one which was in current
use at church services, for it bears a liturgical character, and
is quite foreign to the manner of Paul. At a later time, when
the Epistle was copied in full along with the additional note
to Ephesus, the doxology was retained, and served as an impressive close to the whole work. That the Epistle once
circulated in an abridged form is further attested by the
singular fact that in some manuscripts the words " in Rome ",
several times repeated in the first chapter, are omitted. No
one can doubt, or can ever have doubted, that the letter was
addressed to the church at Rome, for this is the determining
factor in all its thought. But it was now the treasured
possession of the whole church. All Christians were expected
to hold the beliefs set forth in it, and any references that
might seem to confine it to one particular community were
carefully removed.

These vagaries in the transmission of the Epistle are not of
much consequence. They need occasion no misgiving as to
whether the Epistle, as we now have it, is the genuine work
of Paul. They serve, however, to illustrate how it was mis-

understood even in early times. It was regarded as a purely
theological treatise, and everything that connected it with the
man Paul and the actual men and women to whom he wrote,
was deliberately left out. All that seemed to matter was the
exposition of a number of formal doctrines. In all times since,
the Epistle has been studied for the most part from this point
of view. The ideas which Paul employs have been traced to
their sources, his argument has been sifted in all its details,
and hardly any thought has been given to his essential
message. Before we can do justice to his Epistle we must
try to read it as he intended it to be read. He wrote it as
a letter to a definite circle of people whom he wished to inspire
with a new faith in their religion and a fuller sense of their
responsibility as Christians. His theological argument is all
incidental to this main purpose. From first to last his mind
is fixed on those vital truths in the gospel which make it the
power of God unto salvation. When the Epistle is thus read
it may still be accepted as the primary statement of the Christian message. Paul was the greatest of Christ's servants, and
was alive as no other man has been to the inner meaning of
his revelation. "We are ambassadors for Christ," he said,
"as though God did beseech you by us." This is a lofty
claim, but ever and again, as we read the Epistle to the
Romans, we can feel that it is true.

II

COMMENTARY ON THE

EPISTLE

ANCIENT letters all began according to a set pattern; first the name of the writer, then the name of the person addressed, then a word of salutation. " Cicero to Brutus, greeting." Courtesy required that some compliment should follow, and a brief prayer for the reader's health and prosperity. Paul opens his letter in the customary manner, but elaborates each part of the formula and interweaves the conventional phrases with Christian ideas. The two or three necessary lines of introduction are thus extended to a long passage, in which he foreshadows the whole purport of the Epistle that follows.

He makes plain at the outset that he is no adventurer, as his enemies were wont to allege, but a true apostle, entrusted, like the prophets of old, with a divine message. It concerns Jesus Christ, who had lived on earth as a man, but whose higher nature had been manifested by His rising from the dead. As Son of God, He has a claim on the obedience of all men, Gentiles as well as Jews, and the duty of His apostle is to proclaim Him everywhere, as he will shortly do at Rome.

This passage, brief and preliminary as it is, has a crucial bearing on the vexed question of Paul's relation to the earthly Jesus. It has been held that he knew almost nothing of the life of Jesus, but this is absurd when we remember that he was the intimate friend of Peter, and that he had worked hand in hand for many years with Barnabas and other members of the original Christian circle. He must have known a great deal more about the acts and sayings of Jesus than we know

now. So it has been argued that although he had this knowledge he deliberately put it aside, and concentrated wholly on the vision of Jesus risen and glorified. Does he not admit this himself when he says explicitly, " Though we have known Christ after the flesh, yet now we know him so no more "? (2 Cor. v. 16). These words, however, must be taken in their context, " Henceforth we know no man after the flesh." You cannot know any man rightly when you look only at his appearance, his race and connections, his trade or profession. These things are external to the man, and most of our false judgments are due to our stopping short with them, never thinking of what he is in his inner self. Paul had resolved that he would think of Jesus as He had been revealed in His true nature by His death and resurrection and all that He had done for men. He saw that even His earthly life was not intelligible unless it was considered in this light. In the opening verses of Romans, Paul is careful to make clear that this was his position. He believed in Jesus who had lived in the flesh, but had all the time been the Son of God with power.

From himself, the writer, Paul turns to the people whom he addresses. He offers them greeting, not merely on his own behalf, but in the name of God and Christ, for whom he speaks. He tells them that although he has never yet met them, they have been long in his heart, and he has remembered them in his prayers. This is no mere formal language. Paul was the apostle of the Gentiles, and Rome was the outstanding Gentile city. The church in Rome was the standard-bearer in the cause to which his life was devoted, and he could not but think of it constantly and pray that it might have strength for the burden laid upon it. He tells that he had long desired to visit Rome, not merely because this famous city, the very heart of the world, had always had a fascination for him, but because he owed a service to all men; and Rome, the capital of the nations, stood for humanity as a whole. It was the centre of civilization, but Paul, it will be noticed, connects it also with the barbarians. He is coming to Rome for the sake of a world-wide mission, so he includes those who might seem outside the pale.

With this thought in his mind, he proceeds to state the theme of his Epistle. He is the messenger of Christ, and exults in his calling, for he sees in the gospel the answer of God to the world's chief need. What all men are seeking is deliverance. They feel that in this life they are continually under a bondage. What it is they cannot understand, and they think of it in terms of health or society or politics or material surroundings. But all are conscious of something that holds them down, and their one endeavour is to get free. Through Christ, and through Him alone, God has offered them this freedom. It is given by God, and men can receive it only on the condition of faith.

The argument which follows is all to turn on this word " faith " which Paul now throws into the foreground, indicating at the same time what he means by it. The gospel, he declares, is concerned with a righteousness which is given by God, and men have been ignorant hitherto of such a righteousness. They have relied wholly on their own efforts, and in this manner have defeated the power which would have helped them. It has now been revealed that God asks nothing of men but to wait on Him trustfully, receiving what He gives, and this receptivity is faith. God has offered to bestow on us as a free gift what we are struggling to obtain, but we cannot have the gift unless we are willing to receive. This, says Paul, was perceived by the prophet when he declared, "The righteous shall live by faith"—that is, the righteousness which saves is that which comes by faith. We find ourselves in a prison, and the door of escape into a life of freedom is faith alone.

The word " righteousness ", which is ever recurring in this Epistle, has a meaning much broader than that which we commonly attach to it. We call a man righteous when he acts always by a strong sense of justice, and sometimes when we so describe him we wish to suggest that he is wanting in human sympathy, and too conscious of his moral superiority.

Paul means by righteousness that condition of soul which God requires. Men must finally appear before God, and He will judge them according as He finds them in the right condition or the wrong. It is worth observing that " righteous ", to begin with, was only a careless way of saying " rightwise "; that is the spelling found in all English books up to the sixteenth century. When a man is just what he ought to be he is in a state of " rightwiseness ", and it is in this sense that Paul employs the word, in its Greek equivalent. Men have become perverted and diseased, and have sought in vain to recover their health of being. God is willing to do it for them. He has offered them by way of gift that " rightwiseness " which they once possessed and which they have lost through sin.

THE UNIVERSAL NEED   i. 18-iii. 20

With remarkable skill Paul has advanced, almost imperceptibly, from the formal opening to the main subject of his Epistle. He is to show that deliverance is now possible to all men, but before telling how it may be obtained he requires to prove that all stand in need of it, and have been seeking it hitherto by paths which could lead them nowhere. He might have taken his examples from any religion or philosophy or political system which has ever been devised, but he confines himself to the two methods of salvation which were most familiar to his readers—the Greek method and the Jewish. These, he recognizes, are typical of all the others.

So he turns first to the Pagan civilization of his time, based as it was on the art and wisdom of the Greeks. To all appearance it had brought a wonderful freedom to the human spirit. Men had escaped from barbarism, and had forced material things into their service, and attained to every kind of knowledge; but there had never been a time when humanity had become so utterly degraded. Paul draws a lurid picture of the corruption into which the Pagan world had fallen, and it has been argued, not without some truth, that he confuses one small section of society with the whole. In the worst times there are always multitudes of men and women who lead good and honourable lives; they are never heard about, while the bad parade themselves and seem to occupy the whole stage. It was undoubtedly so in the first century, and if it had been otherwise Christianity could never have made its way. But Paul's indictment, while it may be too sweeping, is borne out in the main by the evidence which has reached us from many sources. Vice of every description was rampant in that age as it has never been before or since, and had ceased almost to excite any repugnance. Paul closes his dreadful catalogue with a verse which seems at first sight an anti-climax: " They not only do these things but approve those who do them." This is really the darkest stroke in the whole picture. Not only were all those vices practised but the public conscience was dead, and evil could exhibit itself as if it were good. This is the final and deadliest phase of utter social corruption.

Paul does not call on God to punish this evil society, as he had once dealt with Sodom and Gomorrah. The whole point of the accusation is that the moral infamy is itself the punishment. " The wrath of God is revealed from heaven ": it is manifest to all eyes in the degradation to which humanity has sunk. Paul traces this moral ruin, with profound insight, to a perversion of the religious sense. God had made Himself known to men, in the world of nature and in their own better instincts, but instead of worshipping Him they had trusted to their own wisdom, and put their fancies and speculations in place of God. This had led them into vain idolatries, and finally into a gross blindness to the plainest moral laws. To understand Paul's idea we have only to think of how it has been demonstrated in the awful catastrophe of our own times. Nations which prided themselves on their enlightenment have perished by their mere stupidity. They set up idols of their own in place of God, with the result that all their vision was distorted and they turned the truth into a lie. The wrath of God has been revealed not so much in the visible disaster that has befallen them as in the baseness of mind and spirit. Human nature kept changing itself by one degree after another, into something unclean and bestial. Paul had observed this same process at work in the life of his time, and in the light of what he saw he shows the futility of all efforts to win salvation by our own wisdom. That was the Greek method, and we are falling back on it again in our modern world. We look for a great deliverance which will be brought about by scientific discovery, by a better knowledge of man's mind and body and the conditions of social welfare. These things all have their place, and it is plainly our duty to use the best intelligence which God has given us in the service of God. Paul himself is the shining example of a great intellect working incessantly towards a fuller comprehension of the truth. Yet he is aware that by this method no progress can be made beyond a certain point. We can never hope by knowledge of our own to secure our salvation.

He turns, therefore, from the Greek confidence in wisdom to the Jewish reliance on the Law. He feels himself here on more difficult ground, for the Jews had never tried, like the Greeks, to leave God out of account. They took their stand on a Law which was the expression of God's will, and they might justly claim that in this Law they possessed the means which God had Himself provided for their deliverance. Yet the Law had failed, as Paul could testify from his own experience. He had trusted in the Law, and had followed it from his childhood with passionate devotion, but was bitterly conscious that it had deceived him. Why was it that this Law, which God Himself had given, had not fulfilled its purpose?

The Epistle is largely occupied with this question, but before attempting an answer Paul reminds the Jews that while relying on the Law they had never given it a fair chance. He shows that God is inflexibly just, and has placed the world under an order of causality by which a given consequence must follow on a given act. If you venture into fire, perhaps in a noble effort to rescue a child, you are burned. The fire takes no heed of your intention but looks only to your action, and

Paul impresses on us that this rule must always hold good. People complain that when they have done some foolish thing, without meaning any harm, or even with a generous purpose, they are made to suffer for it. They accuse God of injustice because He has not allowed for their ignorance or for the will behind the deed. But He cannot relax the principle by which He rules the world, and you must stand or fall by what you have actually done. It is shown that this is so even when the consequence of an act does not follow immediately. God is forbearing, and may allow men time to see their folly and repair it before it is too late, but He judges always by the act. If evil acts appear to be overlooked they are not forgotten, and if they are not corrected they accumulate, and result at last in some dreadful disaster. This is how the moral law works out even in this life, and the effect will be fully apparent in the life to come. God will finally render to every man according to his deeds.

Having thus laid down the principle Paul applies it to the Jews. They hold to the Law, and think they will be treated with special favour because they possess it; but the Law requires that they should act by it, and everything depends on this action. There are Gentiles who never heard of the Law, and who yet, by following the higher light within them, have acted on its precepts. God looks only on men's actions, and the blessings promised by the Law will come to those aliens who practise it, and not to the people of the Law who disobey it. Paul thus points out that the Law in which they have put their trust has been nothing but a snare to many of the Jews. They take for granted that as God's own people their position is sure. They announce in magniloquent language that they are the guides of the blind, bearers of the lamp of truth, and when you turn from their professions to their conduct you find that they are the basest of men. Paul admits that in many Pagan cities the name of Jew has become a byword, associated as it is with deeds of villainy. Not only the Jewish race but God Himself has been dishonoured by those unworthy believers in the Law. All that is here said of the Jews may be applied with equal truth to Christians. We speak in almost the very language which he ascribes to the Jews of the moral leadership of the Christian peoples, the enlightenment which is our Christian heritage, but nothing is more fallacious than this confusion between the mere possession of a religion and the practice of it. What you call yourself can make little difference in the sight of God, who looks only at what you do.

It is often asserted that while Jesus calls for practical obedience to God's will Paul lays all the stress on certain doctrines which must be believed. This is a superficial judgment, and must be corrected by a passage like this, which occurs, it must be noted, in the most doctrinal of all the Epistles. Paul's position is essentially that of Jesus. Your professions, he says, may be unimpeachable, but it is your actions which count. The moral law is just as inevitable in its working as any physical law, and all that happens to you will be in strict accordance with your deeds. Everything in Paul that seems to be purely doctrinal must be set against the background of this belief in a moral order which cannot be deceived by anything you merely think or say.

Paul feels, however, that in his strictures on the Jews, who claim to be the people of the Law, he has seemed to cast reflections on the Law itself. It was given by God and expresses His will, but He cannot have meant it only to exhibit His own righteousness over against the sinfulness of men. He imagines a Jew protesting, " If I have proved my inability to live up to this holy Law, why should God condemn me? I have done Him a service by offering my sinful life as a foil to His perfection. The more I fall short of His Law, the more I show forth the glory of His nature as compared with frail humanity." No doubt there were many Jews who argued in this fashion when they were reproached with their evil living, and Paul was himself accused of teaching that the more men sinned the more they gave opportunity to God to display His grace. This charge which was brought against Paul in his lifetime has often been repeated since, and some of his ideas have been so construed as to afford good ground for it. Men who have turned to God after lives of gross wickedness are held up for our special admiration. Their evil has been counted to them almost for a virtue, since it magnified the divine goodness which finally redeemed them. They have themselves dwelt complacently on their former vices, and taken a pride in them, believing that in this way they do honour to God. Paul denies emphatically that there is anything in his doctrine to encourage this frame of mind.

He admits, therefore, that by their possession of the Law the Jews have an advantage over the heathen, much as the educated man has a better chance in life than one who has never been at school. But he declares that the very excellence of the Law makes it ineffectual. It sets an ideal before us which ought to produce the very noblest kind of life, but we find, when we try to live by it, that we fall lamentably short. The reason is that while it holds up those lofty standards it supplies no power by which we may attain to them, and this, in Paul's view, is the fatal defect of the Law. He collects from the Old Testament a number of passages in which men are described as radically evil; their nature has become hopelessly corrupt; in thought and word and action they are alienated from God. These charges, he points out, are contained in the Law itself, and are directed against the people who are under its dominion. Thus the Law confesses, with its own mouth, that it has proved impotent. If the Gentiles with their wisdom have missed the way of deliverance so have the Jews, with their reliance on the Law. It has rendered men even more miserable and helpless than they were before, since it makes them aware that they are sinful, which they never realized while they were in heathen ignorance. If they are ever to escape to freedom they must find some way which has not yet been tried or even dreamed of; and this way has now been disclosed to them in the gospel.

GOD'S ANSWER TO MAN'S NEED iii. 21-iv. 25

At this point Paul enters on the main theme of his Epistle. By their own efforts men have achieved nothing, and have only gone farther astray, but God has revealed His own way of salvation, through faith in Christ. The proof that it is God's way is that it is thrown open to all men. Whenever any good thing is restricted to one nation or privileged class you may be sure that it is doubtful or artificial. When a blessing is truly from God all men are made free to share it. Luxuries are for those who can buy them, but air and sunshine, love and health and joy and the beauty all around us are God's gifts, and are offered to all. So the Christian salvation is given on the one condition of faith. There is no need for some intellectual effort of which only a few are capable, or of elaborate practices which are hard to learn and for which the ordinary man has no time or aptitude. All that is necessary is the simple act by which the heart is opened to God, to receive what He freely gives. It is true that all have sinned, but all can accept this new means of deliverance, in the confidence that it is offered to them by God.

Paul states his idea of the Christian redemption in one of those condensed passages which we sometimes meet with in his writings, and which have been the despair of all expositors (iii. 24-26). When a man is called on to sum up in one sentence a conviction he has arrived at by years of intense thinking, he cannot be perfectly simple. There is so much to say that his thoughts crowd on each other and become entangled. He uses words with a meaning which is clear enough to himself but which he cannot convey to others. So in these verses Paul is trying to declare in one breath a historical fact and its significance, the manner in which it operates and the response which men must make to it, the divine purpose which lay behind it and the reason why God had to act in this way and in no other. Some of these ideas he explains in the discussion which follows, others he only suggests, and leaves us to think out for ourselves. The main drift of the passage is made clear in the closing words. God is just and cannot depart from the great principle which determines all justice. Every act must have its consequence; all evil must result in misery and bondage. Men have all been sinning ever since the human race began, and have heaped on themselves a tremendous burden from which they cannot of themselves find any release. But God has effected their deliverance through Christ. By one supreme act Christ has broken the bonds with which màn has been struggling, and nothing now is required but man's acceptance by faith of what has been done on his behalf.

It has often been argued that Paul might have solved his problem much more simply. Could he not have said in plain words that God forgives sin, and that Christ brought us the message of this free forgiveness? Paul, however, is an honest thinker who never shuts his eyes to unwelcome facts. In his own way he anticipates the modern scientific position that the world is governed by inexorable laws which allow no place for any loophole. All that is done, whether it be good or evil, must find its due recompense, for God is just, and cannot by a mere word arrest the consequence of sin, any more than He can forbid a falling stone to reach the ground. If sin is not to produce its effect there must be some positive act which cancels it, and Paul believes that Christ by His death performed that act. It is unfortunate that the idea of the Atonement has so often been conceived in terms of human passion. God, we are told, was angry with men and needed to be appeased. He was bent on retribution, and Christ offered Himself as the victim in place of sinful men. Paul's language may sometimes suggest this mode of thinking, but when he so speaks it is only figuratively. What he has in mind is a necessity which holds good in the moral as in the physical order. The effect of a cause cannot be prevented except by another cause. God's will to men has always been one of love, but the love is powerless unless something has opposed itself to that force of evil which, in the nature of things, must make for destruction. No mere command of God can hold it back. If He is to show mercy there must first be an act so prevailing that the power of sin is overcome.

Paul announces, and this is the centre of his Christian message, that God has accomplished this act in the death of Christ, and has thereby opened that door of deliverance which men had hitherto sought in vain. They had relied on acts of their own—on their intellectual achievements or their scrupulous obedience to the Law. Conscious of all they had done they were satisfied with themselves and looked for their reward. But Paul tells them that the thing they aim at is utterly beyond their reach. They are matching their human weakness against the divine order, and God Himself must interpose to help them. There is nothing they can depend on but faith—surrender to God, in the confidence that He will save them by His own act. This demand for faith was a new thing in religion, and for this reason both Jews and Gentiles, bound by their old traditions, were doubtful of the Christian message. But Paul perceived that faith, although men had never suspected it, had always been the vital religious principle. The gospel, resting as it does on faith, is no innovation. It does not oppose itself to any endeavour by which men have sincerely sought to find salvation. All that it has done is to bring clearly to light the hidden truth which lies at the heart of all religion.

In proof of this assertion Paul takes the test case of Abraham (chapter iv). The Jews looked back on him as the great father of their race, to whom the Law, with its fundamental rite of circumcision, had first been revealed. As children of Abraham they were born under an obligation to revere the Law. If ever there had been a man who had found favour with God it was Abraham, and he had found it through the Law, which he had bequeathed to them. Paul examines the story of Abraham, and shows that he had proved himself righteous because he had trusted a promise for which he had no security but the bare word of God. " He believed God, and it was counted to him for righteousness." This, it is pointed out, was said of Abraham before there was any mention of his circumcision. While he was still ignorant of anything that belonged to the Law he was declared righteous, on the sole ground of his faith. The seal of the Law was only a confirmation of what he had obtained by faith. Paul argues in the Rabbinical manner, deducing a large principle from an incidental hint in scripture, but the principle, however he arrives at it, is unquestionably true. The forms of religion have value only in so far as they express a heart-felt conviction. Prior to any forms there must be the trust in God, the desire to know and serve Him. So it was with Abraham, and so it must be with every man whose religion is worth anything. Abraham, as Paul goes on to say, was the father not only of the people of the Law, but of all who possess that inner conviction which made him God's servant. Faith is the essential thing, and faith consists in a reliance on God and not on yourself. Conscious that you are blind and weak you believe in a higher Power which is working for you, and will accomplish what is altogether beyond your strength. Paul illustrates this from the story of Abraham. God had promised that he would become the father of many nations, and he was a childless man in extreme old age; but he never for a moment doubted the word of God, who can effect that which to men's eyes appears impossible. And in the example of Abraham Paul sees a symbol and a forecast of the nature of Christian faith. As Christians we also believe that God can create life out of death, that Christ arose from the dead and gives life and deliverance to all who put their faith in Him.

THE NATURE OF THE CHRISTIAN SALVATION   V

Paul has made it plain that faith is the one condition on which we can secure the deliverance offered by God. All other methods have been tried and have failed. They must always fail, for the thing you seek for is one which only God can do, and our part can be nothing more than to throw ourselves on God and accept with a full confidence what He is prepared to give. This truth is inherent in the very nature of religion, and Paul now illustrates it from Christian experience. Addressing a body of Christians he feels that he does not need to argue, but has simply to remind them of what they have known for themselves, ever since they believed in Christ. They have a sense of peace with God. They are aware of His bountiful kindness, now that their hearts are open to receive His gifts. They have a glorious hope for the future, and can trust it since it has begun to fulfil itself even now. To be sure they have much to suffer, but their very sufferings have taught them patience, and through patience they have tested their inner strength, and know that they can rest secure in the unfailing love of God. This has all come to them through their faith. In the knowledge that Christ died for a helpless world they have confidence in a divine love on which they can cast themselves without reserve. A man has sometimes been known to give his life for one whom he greatly honours, but this is rare, and no one dies for the unworthy. Christ died for men when they were lost in their sins, and this was plainly a love of divine nature; none but God could have thought of such a sacrifice. And if the love was so unmeasured, what may we not expect from it? If God so helped us when we showed ourselves His enemies, will He not save us from every peril, now that we are His friends? Not only shall we trust ourselves to His protection, but our service of Him will be a perpetual joy.

Paul follows out this thought that by Christ we have obtained more than a deliverance. It was much to recover freedom, but along with that we have become new creatures altogether, partaking in a new kind of life. In this passage Paul discloses what he means by a "justification" which is ours by faith. The word is borrowed from the law-court, and strictly speaking denotes nothing more than a judge's sentence of acquittal. It has been maintained that Paul has only this in his mind. He thinks of sinful men appearing before God, who in ordinary course would condemn them, but in view of their faith in Christ He pronounces them not guilty. Such an acquittal, it is pointed out, is no guarantee that they are in any way different from what they were. A humane and fair-minded judge will sometimes take account of all the circumstances which make an offence excusable, and declare a man innocent when he is guilty. So when God remits the penalty of sin this does not mean that the sinner becomes righteous. The sin is still there, although the Judge, in His mercy, has consented to overlook it. Paul lays himself open to this criticism, and he might have chosen some better word than "justification", but he takes care to indicate in what sense he uses it. Through faith the life of the believer is completely changed. Not only is he pardoned, but he is enabled to start afresh, with a new and better nature.

In order to enforce this idea Paul goes back to the origin of sin, and he again expresses himself in one of those intricate sentences in which thoughts are so packed together that it is hard to disentangle them from one another. His main conception appears to be this. Sin, which carries with it the penalty of death, laid hold of the human race through Adam, who in his own person was all humanity. Adam sinned against a direct commandment of God, and men could not again sin in that manner until the Law was given. Between Adam and Moses, therefore, sin was unconscious, although it still was active, like a hidden disease, and brought with it the necessary consequence of death. So before they knew their misery, just as afterwards, men were in bondage to sin, and freedom came at last, as sin had done, through the act of one man. But when you compare the two acts you see the difference. The offence of Adam was negative in its effect, while Christ bestowed a glorious new gift. Adam sinned for himself alone, while Christ died to redeem the whole world of men. The judgment incurred by Adam was one of condemnation; the act of Christ was God's declaration that men were now set free. Much of Paul's reasoning in this difficult passage has grown strange to us, but there is no mistaking the central thought, and it is a grand and noble one—the very basis, one might say, of the Christian religion. Good is infinitely more powerful than evil. We imagine, in our suffering and despair, that the good is always helpless before the forces of wickedness, but it stands for the will of God, which is certain in the end to prevail. This is our one hope for the world, that if we can only keep goodness alive it will some day subdue all evil by its intrinsic might. Paul applies this principle to the work of Christ. It counterbalanced the effects of sin, and it did far more. It brought something positive and triumphant into the lives of men. Justified by faith in Christ they were endowed with that better will in the might of which they could overcome.

GRACE AS A TRANSFORMING POWER   vi

Exulting in this sense of what Christ has done Paul is led to a startling theory as to the true function of the Law. Those who clung to it had never doubted that it safeguarded them from sin, but in Paul's view it was intended to increase sin, so that the grace of God, when it was at last revealed, should be more abundant. He means presently to develop this idea, but first of all he answers that accusation which had often been brought against him, and which he has already touched on. It was alleged that by magnifying the grace of God he had encouraged men to continue in sin, so as to receive the grace in larger measure. His answer is, in brief, that the effect of grace is so to change a man's nature that he no longer sins. The power which urged him to sin is broken, and loses its hold on him.

It is unfortunate that the beautiful word " grace ", which is the key to all Paul's thinking, has become a theological one, and is associated in our minds with creeds and controversies. Paul does not use it in any theological sense. It means for him simply the generosity, the delight in giving, which is natural to noble souls. Alexander was once asked why he had bestowed a large present on one who had injured him; would it not have been more just to punish the man? " More just to him," was the answer, " but not just to Alexander." It was in a similar manner that Paul formed his conception of the grace of God. We are not to think of God as doling out His benefits with a pair of scales, but as giving freely even to those who have deserved nothing, for it is His nature to give. Our hope is not in anything we have done ourselves but in that infinite grace of God. We cannot doubt it, for in Christ we have received a marvellous gift, all for nothing, and Paul holds that this evidence of God's grace ought in itself to be enough to change our lives. Even the meanest man, when he receives a benefit instead of the punishment which he expected and deserved, is for the moment shamed out of his baseness. The feeling comes to him that he must try henceforth to be a different kind of man. All generosity has something of this power to transform those whom it touches, and in His supreme act of grace God has not only bestowed a gift but a new frame of mind. The better human instincts are awakened. Sin can be resisted and overcome in the knowledge that Christ died for men when they were unworthy of such a sacrifice.

Paul, however, would go much further. He holds that the change which takes place in the Christian man is not merely one of disposition but a radical change. The believer dies to his old life, and begins again, as if he had not lived before. This new life, as Paul conceives it, starts definitely at the moment of baptism, which is like a repetition in symbol of Christ's death and resurrection. As Christ died and was buried and rose again, so the convert is plunged in the water and emerges a new man. He has re-enacted in his own person the death by which Christ redeemed him, and now shares in the risen life of Christ. The nature which was captive to sin has been destroyed, and gives place to a new nature, which is proof against sin and against death which is the effect of sin. This conception of Paul has given rise to sacramental types of religion, in which the more vital elements in Paul's teaching have sometimes been forgotten. He insisted that salvation is by faith; not by any external, magical process but by the response of your own soul to the gift of God in Christ. Baptism can avail nothing unless it signifies your possession of that regenerating faith. The value which Paul attaches to the rite may be accounted for partly by his own mystical temperament, partly by the feeling of his age, in which visible symbols and the things they stood for were not clearly distinguished. But his ultimate motive must be explained in the light of the whole argument of which the passage on baptism forms a part. He is seeking to show that the change effected by Christian faith is an essential and decisive one. When you become aware of the grace of God you are not merely influenced for a time in the right direction. You break away for ever from the old life, and a new nature is born in you. As God has imparted His grace in one great act, so in the confession of Christ you perform your own act, once for all. You die to sin and are alive to God.

Paul therefore turns from argument and implores his readers to prove by their lives that they have undergone the great change. It is evident from his passionate plea that he did not think of baptism as in some magical fashion renewing a man's nature. It is rather the beginning of a strenuous effort; it secures you a foothold which enables you to put forth all your might, in the confidence that you will not strive in vain. You can believe that by the act of Christ the sinful principle in human nature has now been overcome, and that everything now depends on your own fidelity. Christians are to realize, like people in a liberated country, that the forces which oppressed them—lusts and fears and temptations— have now been vanquished, and that they can follow their true life as free men. Paul appeals again to what his readers have experienced for themselves. Comparing their present with their past they can see that while they lived in sin they were in bondage; they are now ashamed to remember what they once were. They know that freedom came to them in their acceptance of the gospel, and it is apparent in all their actions and in the glorious hope which inspires them that they are indeed free men. Sin is a hard taskmaster, and the wages he deals out are nothing in the end but death. God makes us a splendid gift, which we could never have earned, and it consists of eternal life.

THE TWO LAWS   vii

Paul now returns to his strange assertion that the Law had been given, not to rescue men from sin, but to bring them more hopelessly under its tyranny. It has often been assumed that this whole Epistle is an attack on the religion of the Law, and has lost its value now that the battle between Law and gospel has been fought and won. Thus far, however, Paul has only dealt with the Law incidentally, and he now discusses it because the new principle of faith becomes more intelligible when it is contrasted with that other which was embodied in the Jewish Law. The truth is that Paul had long ceased to be much interested in the Law, and his teaching in Romans would have been essentially the same if he had come to the gospel through Greek philosophy, or through some ethical or social theory of our own day. Whatever his approach he would have shown that man can find deliverance by no effort of his own, but only by the grace of God as manifested in Christ. Yet it was the Jewish religion which he knew best, and he takes it as his chief example of the wrong method of seeking salvation. His purpose is not to attack the Law, but to show positively that salvation must be by the free gift of God.

He begins by pointing out that the Law at one time had a real authority. Men had been placed under this legal system and were bound to live by it. If you profess any religion or code of morals you cannot do less, as an honest man, than take it seriously and act by the standards it offers you. But when a man becomes a Christian the Law loses its claim upon him. Paul illustrates his point by the case of a wife whose husband has died, leaving her free to contract a new marriage. The analogy is not a happy one, and it may be remarked in passing that Paul has little gift for illustration. This is one reason why his teaching often appears so arid when compared with that of Jesus in the Gospels. Jesus was in touch with life and nature, and wherever He looked He saw parables, while Paul has to work them out laboriously, and when he has made them they do not fit. So here he speaks of the husband, that is the Law, as dead, but when he comes to apply his metaphor it is the believer who dies to the Law. No doubt he has both ideas in his mind. When Christ appeared the Law passed out of being, and when a man is baptized in the name of Christ he dies to that old life which was controlled by the Law. The thought, however, would have been clearer without the illustration.

Paul then proceeds to answer the charge that he regarded the Law, which God Himself had given, as an evil thing, provoking men to sin. This, he declares vehemently, was never in his mind. The Law had intensified sin, but only by compelling men to see it as it really is. When there was no Law they had yielded to lower instincts without any sense that they were wrong. It was the Law with its plain commandment " Thou shalt not covet " which made covetousness a sin, and so with everything in our nature that is base. The savage who has never learned anything of moral restraint is happy; misery begins when you know better, and are still enslaved by desires and impulses which are destroying your soul. The sin which you once took lightly now becomes an intolerable burden. So the Law, for the very reason that it stands for all that is just and holy, became man's enemy. It confronted him in his sin with God's express commandment, and made him aware that he was condemned. Through the Law sin revealed itself in its true nature, and now slew instead of merely deceiving. What Paul has in mind is the impotence of the Law, with all its noble injunctions. It tells us that we must do right, but has no power to help us. Our lot would have been happier if we had never known the Law, which only drives home to us the sense of our wretchedness.

In a passage of marvellous psychological insight Paul describes this condition of misery which the Law discloses and can do nothing to relieve. He speaks in his own person and is clearly drawing on his own experience, and it has been much disputed whether he tells us of an inward conflict which still torments him or of one under which he used to suffer when he was still subject to the Law. No doubt he thinks chiefly of a man who knows nothing of the Christian message, but the state of mind which he depicts so vividly is one familiar to everybody, and to the good Christian more, perhaps, than to any other. The truth is that he speaks not so much of men in their relation to the Law as of men in their earthly being, with a nature divided against itself. They belong to a lower world and also to a higher one, and the carnal element in them is constantly at war with the spiritual. So Paul describes the conflict between his two selves. He knows what he ought to do, and desires with his whole heart to do it, but discovers at every turn that he cannot. He sees the right and sincerely loves it, and yet somehow, in spite of himself, he chooses the wrong. His whole life is wasted in doing things which in his better judgment he condemns. This is the tragedy of every human being, and it has never been set forth in such lifelike colours as in this chapter of Romans. Everyone can recognize in Paul's analysis his own condition of inward discord. The two laws in our nature are at constant war with one another, and most often it is the higher one which gives way, although we know all the time that it ought to conquer. It represents the will of God and makes for our true well-being, while the opposing law is that of sin, which is working for our destruction. What we need is something that will support that better will which is overmastered so easily by the sinful impulse. "Who will deliver me from this body of death?" This is the great human cry which finds its answer in the Epistle to Romans. The power we need and apart from which we are helpless is given us, says Paul, through Jesus Christ our Lord, and he tells us what it is and how it works for us in the great chapter which follows.

THE WORK OF THE SPIRIT   viii. 1-27

The argument has hitherto been concerned with faith, that attitude of mind by which alone we can receive the gift of God. The deliverance we are seeking has been wrought for us, and we must abandon all vain efforts to achieve it for ourselves, and put our trust in God and in what He has freely given us. This is the manner in which we obtain all the blessings which are most worth having. To get health you do not need to be always thinking of your bodily condition, and trying one medicine after another; that method, as a rule, defeats its own end. Health comes to you without your knowing when you have good air and sunshine, and obey the great natural laws. Paul applies the same principle in the religious sphere. We desire salvation, but there is no contrivance of our own by which we can secure it. It comes to us unsought when we only believe in God and throw ourselves on His bounty. He gives, and all that we need is the faith which can receive.

It might thus appear as if faith were entirely passive. You are to have no will of your own, and need only stand aside and everything will be done for you. You may even continue sinning and yet feel sure that God, in His boundless grace, will give you everything. That was how many people had understood Paul's teaching, as some do now; and in this chapter he sets himself to explain what he really means. Faith, he declares, is not passive, for its very purpose is to fill you with a new energy. He has just described that miserable state in which a man's true will is paralysed, and now he shows how it is set free and is upheld by an invincible power. Through faith we obtain the Spirit, in the strength of which we can do all things.

We sometimes speak as if Paul, by some process of reflection, and perhaps of borrowing from thinkers before him, had arrived at the theory that Christians are endowed with a mysterious power which he calls the Spirit. This, it is assumed, was one of Paul's novel doctrines, and we must

D

decide for ourselves in the light of our modern thinking whether we can still accept it. Paul, however, is not concerned with a doctrine but with a fact. He takes up a word which had been associated from time to time with strange ideas, but which denoted an experience which is familiar, in some measure, to everyone. You feel, if only for a moment, as if you were lifted out of yourself. You find that you are able to face a difficulty or to realize a truth, in a manner which you thought utterly beyond you. Most of all, after heart-felt prayer, you are conscious of a strength in you which is more than your own. Paul thinks of this higher power as that of the Spirit. He believes that by faith in Christ it comes to us as a lasting possession. Our hearts have been opened to the grace of God, and He can now bestow on us this gift of the Spirit, which enables us to do what was formerly impossible. Faith is therefore a key which unlocks the great source of energy. It brings with it a power which takes possession of our own will, and makes it victorious. The Law could not help us because it was " weak through the flesh "; strong in itself it was useless when imposed on mere earthly beings. It was like a noble sword placed in hands too feeble even to lift it. What men needed was a new energy, a more potent quality of life. Those who are only creatures of flesh cannot serve God, however plainly He may state His commandments. They are bent on the things of this world, and have no capacity for the higher interests. The carnal mind must be changed into a spiritual mind by the entrance into it of the Spirit from above.

Paul describes this transformation which is wrought in the Christian man. He has hitherto spoken of the grace of God as acting quite apart from us. When we were lying helpless a hand was stretched out to save us, and we had only to yield ourselves to this power that delivered us. Now he goes on to show that the outward power is also an inward one, enabling us of ourselves to withstand all hostile forces and attain to that true life which seemed quite beyond our reach. For Paul this is the ultimate Christian mystery—that Christ who once died for us is also within us, changing our nature through that Spirit which dwelt in Himself. As He rose from the dead we also rise into a life which is no longer that of our mortal bodies.

As he contemplates this new life of the Christian Paul is filled with a growing rapture. He declares that those who receive the Spirit are in a real sense sons of God, partaking even now of God's own nature. They were formerly bondsmen, and when they served God it was from motives of fear, and they felt at a distance from Him. They are now aware that He has taken them into His household. This is shown even in the language wherewith they address Him. They call Him " Abba ", repeating in their own prayers the very word which Jesus had used when He communed with His Father. It is the Spirit within which enables them thus to pray, assuring them that they are now on the same footing with Christ, and that His Father is also theirs. And if they have this equality with Christ they can be certain that their present sufferings will have the same outcome. He triumphed and ascended into glory, and the day is coming when they will share in His glory.

As he thinks of this wonderful future Paul has a vision before him which makes all earthly troubles shrink into nothing. He sees the whole creation eagerly awaiting the day when man will enter into his heritage as a child of God. All created things are suffering from an imperfection which has been brought on them by the sin of man. God was their Maker, and had meant that they should remain as when He made them and pronounced them good; but the sin of man had caused a leaven of corruption which infected all things, and it cannot be removed until man is set free. His liberty will involve that of the whole created world, which exists for his sake. It is difficult to attach any literal meaning to this high speculation of Paul, and perhaps he did not intend that it should be taken literally. By means of it he seeks to give expression to three ideas, all of them intensely real to him. For one thing he was conscious, as all great poets and thinkers

have been, of something amiss with the material world. Everywhere there is strife and decay; all things fall short of their
completeness. Again, he realizes that nature and man are
bound up together. Man discovers his own longings and
emotions reflected in the world around him, and feels that the
God who cares for him is also present in his whole creation.
Once more, and this is the central idea of the magnificent
passage, Paul seeks to impress on us the greatness and unique
significance of man. Compared with the majestic forces which
surround him and are able so easily to crush him man appears
to be nothing, and yet it is he who gives meaning to everything else. The chief aim of all God's work is the deliverance
of the human soul. In some way we cannot dream of the
salvation of men will bring about the perfecting of the whole
world.

Paul thus imagines all things as striving forward to the day
when men will be set free, and if this is true even of the
inanimate creation, how much more so of men themselves.
Above all, we Christians are filled with a passionate yearning.
Already we have been given the Spirit, which assures us of the
reality of that higher world to which we aspire, and we look for
the time when with soul and body together we shall enter on
the new life. Our salvation as yet is in the realm of hope, and
a thing hoped for is not the same as one seen: but hope brings
strength and comfort, and enables us to wait patiently for the
hour of fulfilment. And in this interval of waiting we need
not lose courage, for the Spirit supports us and helps us to
endure. Of ourselves we only know vaguely what we are
seeking, and in our prayers we can express nothing plainly,
but the Spirit within us speaks on our behalf in a language
which God will understand. Paul doubtless has in mind
that " speaking in tongues " which was practised in the
early church. It was a form of prayer which consisted of
"inarticulate groanings "—sobs and cries and strange forms
of speech, giving utterance to deep convictions which could
not be put into words. The practice came to be abandoned,
even in New Testament times, but it is still true that the best

part of every true prayer is that which cannot express itself—
the inner sense of God, the faith and aspiration which are
often most sincerely present when the language is most
imperfect.

THE CERTAINTY OF SALVATION viii. 28-39

It has been shown that as yet we can only look forward,
but with the Spirit helping us we can be confident that God
Himself has called us, and will bring us safely to that high
destiny which He has appointed for His people. All seeming
difficulties and oppositions will prove in the end to have
worked for our good if we put our trust in God and His
promise. Paul here touches on an idea which he is to develop
more fully in a later part of the Epistle. He believes that God
has predestined those whom He will save, and that their future
is therefore assured. This is one of the most difficult of Paul's
doctrines and none of them has been so often distorted and
misunderstood, but it is well to note at this point that he thinks
of predestination on the part of God as the grand encourage-
ment of all believers. They are to feel that while they are
weak and changeable God has Himself ordained them for
salvation, and that nothing can defeat His purpose. Since
God has called them He is responsible for their future. They
may think of themselves as already glorified, since what God
has planned He will certainly fulfil.

In the great passage which follows Paul enlarges on this
idea, and at the same time sums up the result of his whole
argument. This is too often forgotten by those who regard
the Epistle as a mere theological treatise, with little bearing on
the real message of Christianity. Paul never for a moment
loses sight of the vital issues. By a winding road of argument
he has been steadily advancing towards this passage, in which
the rapture of Christian faith finds its supreme expression.
He takes up one by one the ideas he has presented in what has
seemed a cold light of reason, and now they glow with life and
passion. It may fairly be said that none of the previous

chapters can be understood apart from this triumphant climax.

He has been seeking to prove that God is with us, and that we may therefore rely on a power which is mightier than any that can oppose us. God Himself has come to our rescue through Christ, and has performed a divine act, which has liberated us once for all. Every other gift is included in that marvellous gift which He has offered us in His Son. Paul imagines a bar of justice where the people of Christ confront all accusers. Whatever the charge may be they can appeal to God, who will declare them innocent. They can leave their cause to Christ, who died on their behalf and now lives for ever to intercede for them. In their earthly life they are beset with many troubles—hardship and persecution and every kind of suffering are heaped on them, so as to make them feel that Christ has forgotten them or is powerless to help them. But they can be confident of His love, which will be with them always. They can bear all calamities, in the assurance that by this road they are marching to victory. No human force can separate them from Christ, and He will also prevail over all the might of the invisible world. Paul thinks especially of that power of fate in which all men at that time believed. We speak to-day of the vast mechanism of physical law in which our human life is hopelessly involved. The ancients meant much the same thing when they thought of man's destiny as determined for him by the stars. Everyone was born under some particular star, and according to its " height " or " depth " at that moment he came to honour or disaster. Paul is convinced that the whole chain of necessity has now been broken. Man has been given his freedom as a spiritual being. He is a child of God, and is subject only to that love of God which is manifested in Jesus Christ.

THE DESTINY OF ISRAEL   ix-xi

A new section of the Epistle now opens, unconnected, it might seem, with the previous discussion. Paul has been speaking of the deliverance which God Himself had effected, after all the struggles of man had failed. His thought has swept over a vast field of human history, and over the past and future of all the created world. Now he takes up a theme which in comparison is a very narrow one. Why has God permitted Israel to reject His message? Long ago He had chosen this people and promised it His salvation, but He has now passed it over, and transferred His gift to the Gentiles. As we turn to this new section of the Epistle we cannot but feel a disappointment. After soaring so high in the chapter which has just closed, Paul seems to fold his wings and drop down suddenly to earth.

It has been argued that the new section is practically a different letter. Paul has finished his real message to the Romans, but while the pen is in his hand he decides to write about a matter which he knows has been perplexing them, though it has nothing to do with his main theme. There may be truth in this view in so far as a letter is not tied down to any strict logical sequence, and Paul could feel himself at liberty to pass over, as abruptly as he pleased, from one subject to a quite different one. We need always to remember, too, that Paul has a special audience in view. If we knew more of the circumstances of the Roman church we should probably find that this enquiry into the place of Israel, which to our minds appears quite irrelevant, had a very definite purpose. Even as it is, when we read between the lines, we can perceive that among the Roman Christians there was a strong bias against the Jews, and Paul may well have felt that this needed to be corrected, or the meaning of the gospel would be fatally misconceived. Our sense that this new part of the Epistle is out of keeping with the other may be due to nothing else than our own ignorance.

In one way, however, there is a real and close connection. Paul takes the great principles he has established and applies them to a particular problem, showing how they hold good in this concrete instance. When the man of science has convinced himself of the existence of some general law he tries to relate it to one set of facts and another. The law appears to be valid for the motions of the heavenly bodies; does it operate also in this piece of matter which he can hold in the palm of his hand?   It is in this manner that Paul turns from his consideration of God's purpose with the world to His dealings with the one people of Israel.   He has shown in the previous chapters that the gospel is the revelation of the grace of God, and that it makes its appeal to all men.   With this conception of it in his mind he examines the case of Israel.   We are not to read the chapters as if they had reference only to the controversy of Jew and Gentile which agitated the church in Paul's day and is now a thing of the past.   In the light of one specific instance we are meant to perceive how the divine purpose fulfils itself in the whole life of the world.

Paul begins by expressing his deep concern for the nation to which he is proud to belong.   One of the charges against him was that he was a renegade, who delighted in maligning his own people and in doing everything he could to injure them.   Such characters appear from time to time in every nation, and make themselves despicable not only to their countrymen but to the foreigners whom they wish to please and flatter.   Paul makes it clear that he is not one of those men.   He solemnly protests, in the name of Christ who knows his inmost soul, that he loves his people.   He is ready to pray, as Moses did, that he might himself be rejected by God if only Israel might be saved.   Not only is he bound to Israel by ties of blood, but he recognizes the unique claims of this nation which God had chosen for His own and to which he had entrusted the true worship and the Law and the promises made through patriarchs and prophets—the nation out of which Christ Himself was born.   Who can think of Israel without thanksgiving to God!   He indeed mourns for Israel which has refused the message of Christ, but he will not condemn the whole nation, or believe that God has cast it off.   The real Israel has always been a small minority. Even among the children of the patriarchs God only chose out certain individuals, and this has been His method ever since. He looks not to physical descent but to special qualities which He found only in a few. Not only so, but He Himself determines who shall have these qualities. Paul instances the Old Testament story of Isaac's twin sons, between whom God made His choice while they were still unborn. In this he sees an illustration of how God deals with men—not according to what they do themselves but according to His own purpose, fixed from all eternity. On this idea of a divine predestination the whole discussion is now to turn.

Paul clearly perceives the moral difficulties in which the idea is involved. In saying that God chooses and rejects men without any regard to their own action, do we not accuse Him of injustice? Paul's doctrine has often been held up as a frightful example of the errors into which he was forced by his logic, and which neutralize all that he teaches of the mercy and love of God. But it cannot be too strongly insisted that the idea of predestination was not a monstrous, artificial theory, for the invention of which Paul must be held responsible. He was only facing, quite honestly, one of the mysterious facts of life, perhaps the most mysterious. Why is it that some men, for no fault of their own, are doomed from their very birth to misery, while others have all good things heaped on them without their asking? We speak in our day of social wrongs, and of chance and heredity and environment. In ancient times men submitted, often with a splendid fortitude, to a blind fatality, which it was futile to resist. Paul is a religious man, and cannot rest in the easy solution that life is all a lottery. Nor can he persuade himself, with the friends of Job, that everything is rightly ordered, and that the outcast and miserable are only suffering the punishment which in some way they have deserved. He has to reconcile the apparent injustice of God's government of the world with his belief in righteousness, and to this end he frames his doctrine. We may be repelled by it, but what of the grim realities which have to be explained? Paul is only seeking to maintain his Christian faith in spite of them, and it may be claimed for him that in some measure he succeeds.

First of all he considers the obvious criticisms of his doctrine and suggests several answers, with none of which he is quite satisfied. He begins by taking his stand simply on the finality of God's will. From several passages of scripture he argues that whatever God wills must be accepted as right. He has mercy on whom He will; He selects others as the objects or instruments of His wrath; and it is not for our human intelligence to judge Him. God is accountable only to Himself, and a thing is right because He does it. You may reply, and countless people have done so, "Why, then, does He condemn and punish when it is His own will which has made us what we are?" But here again the answer is sufficient that it is not for men to question the ways of God. He has framed us for His own purposes, just as the potter moulds his clay, and as vessels of His making we must accept our destiny. So it has been with His treatment of Jews and Gentiles. He has determined that the Jews, as a nation, should be thrust from His favour, so that some of them, along with the believing Gentiles, should enjoy it more abundantly. This was long ago foreseen by the prophets, who declared that God would choose a new people and that only a remnant of Israel would be saved. We can only say that God has so willed it. He decided, in His wisdom, that His former people should wander from the true way of righteousness and that the Gentiles should walk by faith. God has so ordained it, and He must be right.

At this point, however, Paul sees the weakness of his argument (ix. 30-x. 13). God has not rejected the Jews for no other reason than He so willed it. The Jews have had themselves to blame. They were shown God's way of righteousness and refused to take it, preferring a way of their own. It was on this account, and not by any arbitrary decree, that God disowned them. Paul, therefore, laments over his people because they have been wilfully blind. They have clung to their traditional Law after it has lost its value, and when Christ has appeared to disclose the true means of deliverance. Moses had given them the Law under the stern condition that it would not profit them unless they strictly obeyed it. This they have failed to do, and they have not perceived that in the Law itself there was the foreshadowing of another demand which would take its place. Their prophets had warned them that the true religion was an inward one, and that in their own hearts they were to hear the call of God and respond to it by faith. Nothing is required of men which is beyond their power. They have only to have faith in God's message and make a brave confession of their faith before their fellow-men. The Jews had disdained this plain way of deliverance. It was one which all men could follow, and they wished to preserve the distinction between themselves as a privileged race and the Gentiles who were ignorant of the Law. But God had offered His message through Christ for the very reason that all might be able to accept it. As the one God who is over all He acknowledges no distinction between one race and another. His gift is open to all, on the one condition of faith.

A plea is here introduced for more zeal on the part of all believers in the work of diffusing the gospel (x. 14-21). Since it is meant for the whole world those who have received it must make it known, and share their blessing with all their fellow-men. This passage might seem to be only a digression, but it is central to the whole Epistle. More plainly than anywhere else Paul here discloses his purpose in writing as he does to the Roman church. He is coming to Rome in order to make it his starting-point for a new mission, and he needs the co-operation of the Christians in the capital. He and his fellow-missionaries will do the work, but they require to have the church in Rome behind them. This will provide weight and impulse to a movement which will bring new life to multitudes now lying in darkness. Salvation is by faith, and faith is awakened by a message, and the message must be conveyed by messengers, and they cannot go forth unless there are those who will send them. This is the service which Paul

desires of the Roman Christians. They have now the opportunity of earning that welcome which is always given to those
who carry good tidings. To lands which have never heard it
they can offer that gospel of peace which all men have been
waiting for, and which is meant for all. Paul rejoices to think
that the message has already gone forth and that the Gentiles
are eagerly responding to it; but what of the people of Israel?
They also have heard; they were indeed the first to receive
the message; but those whom they despised as ignorant and
heathen have answered the call before them. It might seem
as though God had rejected them, but it is not so. It is they
who have rejected God, although He has pleaded with them to
come in.

Paul thus returns to his theme of God's dealings with His
chosen people (xi. 1-24). In spite of His promises to them
He appears to have cast them off, but this cannot be, for God
is always true to His word. If any proof is needed of God's
continued care for Israel it is supplied by the case of Paul
himself, for he belongs, as he now affirms more emphatically
than before, to the authentic Hebrew stock, sprung as he is
from the tribe of Benjamin, which in times past had ruled
over the others. In his own person, too, he is a living evidence
that there are some in Israel who have gladly received the
message. Such Israelites there have always been. Elijah had
complained in his day that of all the people he alone had
been faithful, but God had assured him that he was only one
of seven thousand. This is no less true in the present.
Among all the faithless in Israel there are many whom God
has singled out as His servants. They cannot break away
from Him, for He has chosen them of His own grace, and
they are under His protection. Israel as a nation has been
unbelieving, and God who predestines all things must have
willed it so. Prophets and psalmists had acknowledged in
their own time that there were many whom God had permitted to close their eyes and who seemed to be excluded
from any share in His blessing. Yet there had ever been
those who knew God truly and served Him. In the worst

of times He has set apart this remnant of faithful souls, chosen
and guarded by Himself. Why is it that God has acted
in this strange manner, allowing the mass of His people
to be blinded, while He has granted the true insight to a
few?

So we are thrown back again on the mystery of predestination, but Paul looks at it now with a new understanding, in the light of what has happened to Israel. When
he considered it in the abstract he could only say that God
does whatever He pleases, and that what He does must be
right. If a man should act in that arbitrary fashion we should
certainly call him unjust, but our human standards cannot
apply to God. We are only the clay in His hands, and He
is free to make of us what He will. Paul cannot be satisfied,
however, with this reasoning. If we believe in God at all
we can be sure that when He appears to act unjustly this is
only due to our ignorance. Our range of vision is narrow
at the best, and if we saw farther we should perceive that
behind all His actions, to our eyes so meaningless, there is
some wise and just purpose. This, for Paul, is made evident
by the example of Israel. God had apparently caused His
people to fall away, but this does not mean that He had
abandoned them. Their refusal of the gospel had impelled
the church to turn to the Gentiles, and the faith of the
Gentiles will sooner or later react on the Jews themselves,
and bring them to a right mind. By their temporary fall they
had secured a blessing for the whole world, and when once
again they share in God's favour, as they will some day do,
they will become in a far larger sense His people. So Paul
declares that in his work for the Gentiles it is the welfare of
the Jews he is seeking. He throws his whole heart into this
mission to strangers in the confidence that by saving them
he will save at least some of his own countrymen. As yet it
is only a few who are able to respond to him, but these first-
fruits give promise of a rich harvest. And when all Israel is
gathered in God will fulfil His great purpose for the world.
Israel was helping it on even when seeking to thwart it.

When Israel joins whole-heartedly in working for it, there will be new life for all mankind.

It is not hard to grasp the idea which underlies this argument, at first sight so complicated and fanciful. A small, immediate end is often best attained by aiming at a larger one. To gain prosperity for yourself you have first to see to it that the whole community is prosperous. To effect some minor reform you must work for the larger principles of liberty and justice, and when these are secured the little improvement will come of itself. Paul interprets the action of God by this rule. It might seem as if God had forgotten His own people when He left them alone and was intent wholly on the saving of the Gentiles; but it was necessary even for the saving of Israel that the larger world should be saved first. There could be no blessing for the one nation until a great movement was in process for the good of all nations. When a ship is stranded little can be done by tugging at it with the boats. The sailors are content to wait patiently until the tide sets in from the ocean, and lifts them out of the shallows. So Paul looks forward to the fullness of the Gentiles. When this has come in, and the world's whole life is raised to a new level, Israel also will be saved.

Here again Paul interrupts his train of thought with a special appeal, the force of which would no doubt be clearer if we knew more of the situation at Rome. He has spoken of the Gentiles as alien branches grafted on the stem of Israel in place of natural branches which have been cut away. He now warns the strangers who have been thus favoured that they must not be boastful and self-confident. God has not been gracious to them for any merit of their own. If Israel has lost its privilege this will happen to the Gentiles also unless they keep steadfast in their faith, which is their one claim to the bounty which God has shown them. They need to think of their position as still a doubtful one. If God has rejected His own people in their favour will He not gladly take them back when they are duly penitent? The goodness of God must not make us forgetful of His severity to those who presume too much on His grace. It may be gathered that the Gentile section of the Roman church was now in the majority, and was inclined to be cold or patronizing towards the Jewish members, without whom it would never have come into exist-ence. Ill-feeling to the Jews had always been strong at Rome, and at the time when Paul wrote it was suspected, on good grounds, that Palestine was preparing for revolt. It may well be that the political feud had affected relations within the church, and that Christians were now anxious to disown or belittle the Jewish origins of their religion. Paul takes care to remind them of their debt to Israel, which in spite of all that had happened was God's people. Some years before, when he had stood almost alone against a powerful Jewish opposi-tion, he had denounced the Jews unsparingly. Now, when it was they who were in disfavour, he pleads their cause, although he knew that by doing so he risked the resentment of the Roman church, which he was so anxious to please. Nothing that he ever wrote is more characteristic of the generous spirit of Paul than this defence of his former enemies.

After the brief digression he returns to his theme, and now offers his final explanation, not only of the rejection of Israel, but of the whole mystery of God's government of the world (xi. 25-36). He declares that the fall of Israel is only for a time, and is intended to serve a great divine purpose. Part of the nation has been blinded in order that all of it may some day see the light, and not only all of Israel, but the whole out-lying world. The deliverance of Israel is not possible without this larger redemption. God indeed made a covenant with His people, and promised them His salvation, but He could not keep His promise until He had first, to all appearance, turned against them. This was the only means by which He could bring the Gentiles to a knowledge of the truth, and through the salvation of the Gentiles He meant that Israel also should be saved. He has been faithful to His promise. He never recalls a gift or rejects anyone whom He has chosen. But He effects His purpose in His own way, withholding His mercy sometimes until it can extend itself more largely, and thus flow back in richer measure on those whom He seems to have abandoned.

This idea of Paul is no mere pious imagination. History is full of instances of nations which, in their ignorance or folly, have allowed some prize to pass to others, and have yet, through the example of those others, more than recovered what they had lost. Paul's own prediction of the future of Israel may yet come true, and in some measure has already done so. In disowning their supreme Messenger the Jewish people missed their opportunity, but his message was welcomed by the lands which lay in darkness, and through them has become a living power in the life of the Jews. A day is surely not far off when they will be one family in a larger humanity, which will know no distinction of Jew or Gentile, bond or free. This, as Paul sees it, is the ultimate plan which God is fulfilling through Christ.

He thus concludes with a glowing passage in which he sets forth what he holds to be the true meaning of predestination. It might seem as if God is unjust in choosing some and rejecting others, in driving the mass of men into unbelief that He may reserve His mercy for a few. But He finally rejects nobody. He is working on a vast plan, which as yet we cannot understand, whereby all men will share at last in His salvation. It must here be observed that in ordinary Calvinistic doctrine Paul's idea of predestination has been cruelly misrepresented. He has been supposed to teach that even the devoutest Christian cannot be sure of his standing with God. He may believe in Christ and practise every Christian virtue, but everything depends on whether his name is written among the elect, and this he can never know until the day when the books are opened. Thousands of the holiest men and women have passed their lives under a dreadful fear that after all they may have toiled in vain. God's mercy is only for those whom He has chosen, and who they are can be known only to Himself. Paul himself is not responsible for this inhuman doctrine. He takes for granted that all Christians are among the elect, and have become Christians for no other reason than that God has chosen them. Again and again he addresses his readers as "elect of God", "called to be saints". Faith in Christ carries with it the certainty that you have obtained God's mercy, and the Christian must never doubt himself, for God will sustain with His own power those whom He has chosen.

Paul had begun, then, with explaining predestination from the sovereignty of God, who can do whatever He pleases, since His will is the ultimate law. Now the mystery has been probed more deeply. God acts according to His will, but His will is one of infinite wisdom and love. From the beginning He has prepared man's salvation, and has been working out His purpose in ways that are beyond our knowledge. To our human intelligence all seems arbitrary and meaningless. We lie at the mercy of blind forces which take no account of the justice and goodness which we attribute to God. Yet all the time He is fulfilling His great plan. When He appears to have forgotten it, this is only because it is infinitely larger in scope than we can comprehend. No one can fathom the mind of God. He is Lord of the universe and His action is on a boundless scale, while we cannot see beyond our narrow horizon. We can only believe that He has a purpose, and that it is one of eternal love.

Paul thus speaks the final word on what must always be the most baffling of all problems. He did not in some wilful mood invent the harsh doctrine of predestination, which now, in our more enlightened day, we can set aside. He was confronted with a fact, which we may call by various names, but which forces itself upon us in ever more terrible forms as we understand more of that mechanism of necessity in which man's earthly life is involved. Questions arise to which there can be no other answer than this one which is offered by Paul. The ways of God are inscrutable, but we can trust His purpose, and since He is God, whose will is revealed to us in Christ, His purpose must be one of love.

E

It is Paul's custom to close every Epistle with a few
practical counsels. They seem at first sight to be added by
way of postscript after he has finished the main subject of
his letter, but when they are examined more closely they are
seen to be vitally connected with it. The study of some purely
religious question has led of its own accord to a consideration
of how it bears on common duties and perplexities. In
Romans the practical section is much fuller than in any other
Epistle. It is also more clearly related to the preceding
discussion, in which Paul has impressed on his readers the
nature of the Christian message. Having shown them what it
is, in its essential principles, he now points out how they
must give effect to it in their daily lives.

The section is arranged carefully in three parts. The first
one deals with the broad moral duties which are incumbent
on all Christian men. The second is concerned with civil
obligations. Paul cannot forget that his readers are in Rome,
under the very eye of the imperial power which has now
grown suspicious of the Christian movement. How are they
to behave as good citizens and yet stand true to their religion?
In the third section he thinks of them as members of a
Christian community. He knows that dissensions have arisen
in the Roman church, and that each party is stiff in its own
opinions, and seeks to override the others. Can they not
realize that they have one Master, and that His different
servants must be left free to serve Him as He Himself requires?
This is the very meaning of fellowship in the church.

The Christian Spirit in Action. xii

As he begins his counsels Paul takes care to indicate that
they follow inevitably on what he has said before. God has
done everything for men and therefore they must serve Him
with their whole being. In former times the worshipper had
laid on the altar something which he valued, but which was
yet external to himself. The Christian sacrifice must be one

of actual living, one of mind and personality. God has set us free from bondage to this world, and we must show by all our conduct that we have indeed entered on a new life, and are bent solely on doing the will of God. So Paul proceeds to show that the chief hindrance to the higher kind of life is an over-estimate of oneself. We often speak of vanity as if it were only a harmless folly, but more than anything else it distorts the vision, and disables us from performing the duty for which God has fitted us. Paul illustrates this from those jealousies in the church with which he was so painfully familiar. Instead of acting like the different parts of one body, each confining itself to its own function, he found Christian people everywhere neglecting their proper tasks and attempting, out of sheer vanity, to perform the tasks of others. The first condition of all usefulness is to know your own special gift, for you may be sure that God has granted you one, or you would not be an individual person. You cannot discover your gift unless you think first of God's demands, and forget your obtrusive self. So Paul reminds his readers of the wide range of service which is open to them. There is something which everyone can do if he will only cease envying and grudging other people, and uses his own talent in the common cause.

Each one has his special work, but there are some qualities which all must cultivate, whatever their work may be. These qualities belong to the new type of character which is formed in a man when he is justified by faith and has received the Spirit. The Christian must have that genuine love for others which condemns that which is evil in them and encourages that which is good. He must be brotherly to all and willing that honours should go to his neighbours rather than himself. He must never slacken in his zeal, but serve Christ constantly, with the fire of the Spirit glowing in his heart. With a glorious hope before him he must bear up through all trouble and persevere in prayer. In his dealings with other men he must be generous and hospitable, forgiving those who have injured him, in sympathy with his friends in their joys and sorrows.

He must live in harmony with all men, and must not despise the lowliest duties. However men may act towards himself he must never wrong them in return, but set the world a clear example of an honourable life. As he closes this beautiful description of what the Christian man should be Paul comes back to the primary need for a peaceable, forgiving spirit. This is the very mark of a true Christian—that for his part he has a quarrel with none. He leaves it to God to recompense the evil doer, and the only revenge he takes on his enemy is to treat him with kindness when he finds him distressed. The best victory over evil is to answer it with good.

The Christian as a Citizen.   xiii

At the time when Paul wrote the feeling had arisen that Christianity was dangerous to the state. A cry had been raised on the streets of Thessalonica, just after Paul had first appeared in Europe, " These men do contrary to the decrees of Cæsar, saying that there is another King, one Jesus " (Acts xvii. 9). This belief that the new religion was political in its aims had now grown in strength, and Christians everywhere were liable to trouble at the hands of the civil authorities, and most of all in Rome itself. Not unnaturally, like all minorities which feel themselves unjustly treated, they were apt to retaliate, and apparently this had happened at Rome. We can gather from Paul's admonitions that the Christians had taken up the attitude of passive resistance, and were affording some real ground for the suspicion that they were bad citizens. Paul advises them to submit cheerfully to the laws under which they live. He tells them that earthly rulers are appointed by God to enforce justice and right conduct, and that no one whose actions are blameless has anything to fear. The Christian must be even more careful than other men to be law-abiding and to pay his taxes and respect all officers of state.

The course advised by Paul was obviously wise and necessary if the church was to be left unmolested, and it has sometimes been held that his counsels in this chapter are merely prudential. He takes pains, however, to make it clear that he had other motives. Good citizenship, he declares, is a matter of conscience, a genuine religious duty. He does not hesitate to say that the civil power stands, in a sense, for God Himself, and that submission to it is a real part of man's obedience to God. The first law of God's universe is order. He orders the motions of the stars and the tides of ocean, and the men who preserve order in a kingdom or a town or a business are to that extent doing God's work, and those who profess to serve God must support them. It may be that Paul pushes his rule too far. His words have been quoted time and again in defence of tyrants and iniquitous systems, and have been offered as an excuse by many Christians who were too timid or indolent to stand up against crying abuses. Paul himself, it must be admitted, sadly misjudged the purity of Roman government, which was shortly afterwards to condemn him to death by the laws which he here approves. Yet his principle in itself is true and far-reaching, and is too much forgotten in many of our modern presentations of Christianity. It is the religion of brotherhood, but it is also the religion of order, and if order is not enforced love and goodness and forgiveness will be of little avail. Paul called for submission even to a pagan government because it was trying to promote some kind of harmony in a chaotic world. He made his demand in virtue of his office as a Christian Apostle, for any power that brings order out of confusion is working in the cause of Christ.

His counsel to obey the civil authority merges in others of a more obviously religious kind. One of a man's primary duties as a member of society is to pay his debts, and this the Christian must do; but there is one debt which is never cancelled, however often it is paid, and that is love to your fellow-men. Love is, indeed, the substance of all laws. Their one aim is to compel that consideration of others which you practise spontaneously when you love them. Paul has urged his readers to be good citizens, but he reminds them in closing that the great requirement, in social and political matters as in all others, is to have more of the Christian spirit. The time is drawing ever nearer when Christ will return to judge the world. Let His followers have done with all low desires and appetites, with all practices which cannot bear the light, and make ready to meet Christ at His coming. According as they have His mind in them they will rise above their lower nature and all its temptations to wrong. It was on these verses that the eyes of Augustine happened to fall, when he was bidden by an inner voice, in the great crisis of his life, to lift the book and read.

The plea for a higher spirituality arises, it will be noted, out of a discussion of civic duties. We are coming to see more and more clearly in these anxious days that all our political problems are, in the last resort, moral and religious. Types of government, social reforms, economic adjustments will of themselves help us little. What is needed is some change in the minds of men. We must understand the real ends of life. We must learn to think differently of ourselves and of our fellow-men, and acknowledge some moral authority which is above all laws. Almost daily some new project for a better society is put before us, but always with the proviso that on both sides there must be a spirit of goodwill. As a rule this is thrown in incidentally, but it is the one thing that really matters. No plan will ever succeed when the goodwill is wanting, and when it is present the right plan comes usually of its own accord. How can men's minds be so changed that they will think kindly and justly of one another and look constantly to the common good? This was Paul's question, and it is our question still, and there is no real answer to it but that which Paul found in the gospel.

The Strong and the Weak. xiv-xv. 13

From life in the state Paul now turns to life within the church itself. After his custom he does not treat the subject in a loose general way, but keeps his mind on the particular church he is addressing. A church is made up of a group of people who feel themselves to be brothers in Christ; was there anything in the Roman church which stood in the way of this brotherhood? Paul had heard of one cause of division which was all the more harmful as it affected daily intercourse, and fostered a sense of arrogance in one party and of inferiority in another. There were some who had cast off the old scruples concerning food and drink and sacred days and seasons. They were proud of their broadmindedness and called themselves "the strong", in contrast to "the weak", who still believed that it was wrong to eat certain kinds of meat and neglect the observance of holy days. It has been assumed that the two parties were simply those of Gentiles and Jews, but Paul says nothing to indicate this, and the division was probably on different lines. All ancient religions made much of outward practices, and among Gentile converts there would be many who were still troubled with doubts when they were offered a food previously forbidden, or were tempted to disregard a day they had always held sacred. Paul's own sympathies were with the "strong", and he is careful to make this evident. He knows, as a Christian, that no outward thing is in itself defiling, and that the service which God requires is an inward and spiritual one. Yet here he takes sides with the "weak". He lays down the rule that a man must always be true to his own conscience even in trivial things and that he must also respect the conscience of his neighbour.

He declares, therefore, that if you have thrown off the old inhibitions, as you have a perfect right to do, you are not to quarrel with the man who obeys them, and much less despise him. Neither must you sit in judgment on the other man, for God acknowledges you both. A servant is only responsible to his master, and if he is trying honestly to do his best his master will support him. One man thinks that he will please God by abstaining from certain foods, another by eating them. If the motive of both is to please God, they are both right. The one criterion is that in all things you look beyond your own wishes and the judgments of other men, and do what God demands of you, and in this your conscience must be your guide. Paul here lays down a principle which has often been misunderstood. "No man," he says, "lives to himself or dies to him-self." This is commonly taken to mean that your acts are never merely personal, but have an effect on other lives, which you need to consider as well as your own. No doubt this is true, but Paul's meaning is that you must think neither of yourself nor of other men, but simply of God's command to you. In life and death you belong to Him alone, and this makes you independent of all human censures. We are en-trusted with our own lives, and must live them bravely and freely, knowing that God is our only Judge, and that each of us is responsible to Him alone.

Paul is thus led to affirm the great principle of individual liberty. The question of meats and drinks which he discusses is itself a trivial one, but he lifts it, as his manner is, to a higher level, and arrives at an answer which can never lose its sig-nificance. The church has been tempted in every age to pre-scribe for all its members what they must do and believe, and it is curious to note that the church at Rome, even in its earliest days, was claiming this authority. Pressure was put on all who belonged to it to conform in everything to the pre-vailing custom. This was not Paul's idea of a church. He was himself in full agreement with the dominant party at Rome, and in past years he had vehemently insisted on his Christian freedom with regard to meats and drinks and holy days. But he now feels it more important that he should not interfere with the freedom of others. By trying to impose his own view on those who thought differently he would defeat the whole purpose of the church, which was to unite in one brotherhood all who had the personal faith in Christ. If you denied them individual freedom you might have a disciplined army, moving at the word of command, but not a Christian church, in which everyone counted separately as a child of God. Not only so, but Paul saw the moral danger of meddling with another man's conscience. What you oblige him to do may be to your mind perfectly innocent, and your judgment may be right. But he sees the matter differently, and while he does what you require he believes that his action is wrong.

In this he may be mistaken, but that does not alter the fact that he violates his conscience and thereby sins. The very essence of sin is to oppose God's will by doing what He has forbidden you. On two grounds, therefore, Paul pleads for mutual tolerance. There must be harmony in the church, and this cannot be unless men of different opinions are willing to work together. There must also be personal conviction. Faith is the watchword of Christianity, and faith is worth nothing unless it is our own. However a man acts under compulsion he cannot be right so long as he has an inward doubt. " Whatever is not of faith is sin."

It may fairly be argued that Paul concedes too much to the individual conscience. There will always be those who object to any measure, however right and useful, for reasons which appear to them morally imperative. Must the majority hold back because of the misguided conscience of a few? Is there not a point at which the most honest scruples must be overruled in the general interest? It must be noted, however, that Paul does not advocate any submission to the narrow-minded. On the contrary he holds emphatically that the strong must obey their consciences as well as the weak. There will always be differences among Christian men, and every man must hold firmly to what he feels, in his own mind, to be right. But he reminds us, and this is the central point in his argument, that the essential things are righteousness and peace and joy in the Holy Spirit. It is on these great common interests that stress must be laid, and when they are kept in the forefront the things which separate us fall into their place, and cease to trouble us. Full liberty may be granted to every conscience so long as our minds are steadfastly fixed on those higher ends, which belong to the very substance of the Christian faith.

So Paul closes his warnings to the divided church with a practical exhortation. Those who cannot think alike are not to censure and condemn each other, but should be mutually forbearing, and try to work together. If you count yourself among the strong this only means that you should help the weak and carry the heavier end of every burden. This is how

Christ Himself acted. The prophet had rightly foretold that
when men reproached Him He would take it patiently and
never relax in His work of helping them, and from this scripture, so amply fulfilled in the life of Christ, we must learn our
own duty. Patience is God's own gift to us, and when we
feel resentful towards those who thwart us we must pray for
more patience, so that we all may live in harmony. Whatever
our differences we are servants of Christ, and can join together
in the worship of God who is the Father of Christ, and our
Father through Him. He receives us as brethren, and we
ought so to receive one another.

The Need for a Wider Mission.   xv. 8-13

With one of his subtle transitions Paul merges his appeal
for unity among the Roman Christians in a new plea for
their co-operation in the great work to which he has set
himself. This has been his main object in writing the letter,
and now as he closes his whole argument he sums it up by
dwelling on its practical import. Christ came to the Jews to
reveal the one way of salvation. Although they had rejected
Him He had confirmed the promises which God had made
to their fathers, and had enlarged the scope of those promises
so that they now embraced the whole world. Scripture, when
it is rightly understood, is full of this hope that the Gentiles
would some day share in the knowledge of God and in the
mercy He has ever shown to His people. Isaiah had expressly
foretold that the coming Son of David would establish His
reign over the Gentiles. He would not confine Himself to
any chosen people, but all nations would put their trust in
Him. Paul thus impresses on his readers the universal scope
of the gospel. They had received it themselves and would
be false to their call if they did not help to proclaim it to
the peoples beyond. In the confidence that they will take
their share in this great work Paul makes his prayer for the
Roman church that it may have before it a grand and joyful
future. Three times in the final verse he repeats the word
" hope ". God has done much already for this church, but it

must look forward, assured that He is preparing it, by His Spirit, for a still more glorious task.

PAUL SPEAKS OF HIMSELF   xv. 14-23

It is Paul's custom at the end of a letter to say something about himself and his circumstances and prospects. This is the more natural in the present letter, written at the great turning-point in his career, when he could not but think of what lay before him. He was writing, moreover, to a church which did not know him personally, and needed to be informed on matters familiar to his own communities. The passage is invaluable for our knowledge of the life of Paul. He describes in it, more fully than anywhere else, the nature of his mission, and incidentally reveals much of his own character, and of the motives which inspired him.

He begins by explaining again, in more detail, why he has written the Romans this long letter. He is well aware that they have teachers of their own, on whose counsel they can depend, but his object has been simply to remind them of truths they know. As an Apostle, ordained to work among the Gentiles, he has to make sure that all Gentile churches are fully grounded in the principles of their faith. He has earned the right to speak, for he has laboured much in the common cause. To be sure he has only been an instrument and has no power of his own to boast of, but by word and deed he has spread the gospel widely through the Gentile world. From Jerusalem to the shores of the Adriatic he has proclaimed his message, and the Spirit has attested by many signs that he worked in the name of God. It has been his rule never to go where a field had been prepared by other teachers, but always to break new ground, and for this reason he had hesitated to visit Rome. Now, however, he has done all that he could in the eastern half of the empire, and has planned to travel westward. His aim is to open a mission in Spain, and on his way he will make a sojourn in Rome, which he has longed to do for many years. He looks forward to the Roman Christians escorting him some little way on his farther journey, but he wishes first to make their acquaintance and enjoy something of their company. In the meanwhile he has another enterprise before him. For some time past he has been collecting a sum of money in Macedonia and Greece for the relief of Christians in Palestine, whom he knows to be in poverty. The Greek churches have indeed been generous, although they have only paid their debt to the mother-church from which they had received the gospel. He is now conveying this gift to Jerusalem, and after he has performed this service he will start on the long journey to Spain, by way of Rome. He cannot doubt that this Roman visit will be rich in blessing for the cause of Christ.

Paul was indeed destined to visit Rome, but not in the manner he had planned. He was to make the journey as a prisoner, and to die by the headsman's sword in the city he had so ardently wished to see. His dream of a great western mission was never to be fulfilled, and some premonition of the tragic end seems to come over him as he writes the concluding verses. He begs his readers in the name of Christ to pray earnestly on his behalf. They are to pray that the mother-church will accept his peace-offering, for he was still uncertain whether old quarrels had been forgotten. In this respect his fears were to prove groundless. But he also had reason to believe that his Jewish countrymen, who had long detested him, would make some attempt upon his life when he ventured into their stronghold. Knowing his danger he asks to be commended to God's protection. He has been speaking confidently of his far-reaching plans, but now at the last he confesses that all is uncertain and that he can only trust himself to the will of God. So the final verses are charged with a deep emotion, and this reflects itself in the parting benediction, which is brief and simple, although it closes the longest of Paul's Epistles. " May the God of peace be with you all."

AN APPENDED LETTER   xvi

There are many reasons for regarding the last chapter of Romans as a separate note, attached by accident to the main Epistle. While he stayed at Corinth, with time on his hands, Paul may have written several letters, of which his secretary made copies. These would be preserved by the local church, and since they lay together and were evidently in the same handwriting, it was natural to assume that they were connected. The benediction at the end of the fifteenth chapter is clearly intended to close the Roman letter, and this additional chapter is written in quite a different tone. Paul is no longer deferential, as to a church which he is addressing for the first time. He now feels at home with his readers and speaks to them familiarly and mentions a large number of them by name. If he was on such friendly terms with so many of the Roman Christians it is difficult to see why he has hitherto written as if he only knew them from a distance.

The chapter consists of a note of introduction for Phoebe, who is preparing to leave Cenchreae, a suburb of Corinth, for another city. Two or three sentences are enough for this testimonial, but Paul takes the opportunity of sending his good wishes to his many friends in the unnamed city. From many indications it appears to be Ephesus. Paul had been working there for several years, and had left only a short time before. His Ephesian friends were fresh in his memory, and he wants them to know that he is still thinking of them. The book of Acts is strangely silent on Paul's life in Ephesus, and we have no means of identifying the obscure names which fill the chapter. We do know, however, that Aquila and Priscilla were his chief assistants in Ephesus, as they had previously been in Corinth, and he mentions them first in his greetings, and with special affection. Nothing is said to suggest that they had changed their place of residence since he had last seen them. Next to them he names Epænetus, the first convert in the province of Asia, again pointing to Ephesus, the capital of the province. It is significant, too, that he is acquainted not only with the persons he salutes by name but with the groups around them. He singles out one and another who holds a Christian meeting in his house, and knows the people who are accustomed to attend it. He could not have this detailed information about Christians in Rome.

It may be assumed, then, that Paul wrote his letter of introduction to the church at Ephesus. He asks that Phoebe should be cordially welcomed and assisted in every way she may require. In her last position she had proved herself a highly capable worker, and Paul takes care to add that he had himself benefited from her help. It is no doubt partly to ensure her a warm reception that he makes her the bearer of greetings to his old friends. Of all the people he mentions we hear elsewhere of only two, but the list, with its accompanying notices, is highly interesting and throws many side-lights on conditions in a primitive church. We can see, for one thing, that the membership was very miscellaneous. The names are Jewish and Greek and Latin. Some of them were customary names of slaves; others denote people of some wealth and standing who were able to accommodate little gatherings in their homes. This house-gathering was an important feature in the early church. As yet the Christians could afford no regular buildings, and they would not have been permitted to make this public display of their religion. They worshipped in the court-yard of some large house, and when their numbers increased they divided into groups, each with its own house of meeting. Another thing which is noticeable in this list of church-members is the prominence of female names. Paul singles out the people on whom he had most depended in his work at Ephesus, and the women take an equal place with the men. His attitude to women has often been sadly misunderstood. He objected to their speaking in public, which would have offended ancient ideas of decorum and brought a bad name on the church; but no one appreciated so much as he did their gifts as teachers and active workers. The short letter before us is a testimonial for a deaconess. It introduces her to a church in which women played a leading part, as they no doubt did in all the churches which Paul had founded.

The persons who head the list of salutations are Priscilla and Aquila, and it is worth observing that Paul names the wife before the husband. The two were probably the most loved and valued of all Paul's associates. He had come to know them at Corinth as tent-makers like himself, and had made his home with them. They had gone by his direction to Ephesus, and had stood by him at a very critical time when, as he tells us in 2 Cor. i. 8-10, he was actually under sentence of death. We can gather, from the terms of his greeting, that his life on that occasion was only saved by the brave intervention of his two best friends. Another very interesting reference is to "Andronicus and Junias, my kins-men and fellow-prisoners, who were in Christ before me". When he describes them as his kinsmen he may only mean that they were Jews like himself, but it is quite possible that they were related to him in a closer sense and that his own conversion was in some way assisted by that of these kins-folk who had already seen the light. The name Rufus is found in the Gospel of Mark, where Simon of Cyrene, who bore the cross of Jesus, is called the father of Alexander and Rufus, men who were evidently well known in the Christian community. The name, however, was not an uncommon one, and the allusion to "their mother and mine" is only another way of saying that Paul honoured the mother of Rufus as if she were his own. To his own salutations Paul adds those of "all the churches of Christ". This is more than a formal compliment, for he writes after the arrival of the various delegates who were to accompany him to Jerusalem. Know-ing that Phoebe was on her way to a sister church they would all wish to be included in the greetings she carried with her.

Paul adds to his salutations some words of warning which confirm the assumption that we have here a note to Ephesus. We learn from the book of Acts that on his voyage to Jerusalem a few months later Paul met the elders of Ephesus at Miletus, and as he parted with them bade them beware of false teachings which threatened to divide the church (Acts xx. 28-30). Here he expresses the same anxiety in much the same words. His readers must be on their guard against those who are creating discords, arguing in plausible language against the message he had taught, with no end in view but their own advantage. He cannot doubt the loyalty of his people, but thinks it wise to offer this caution, for he would have them " wise unto that which is good and simple concerning evil ". They cannot have too much intelligence, but it should be directed wholly towards knowing what is right.

A benediction follows which is meant to close the letter, but a postscript is added with some further greetings. One is from Lucius, who may be our evangelist Luke, another from Erastus, who is described as treasurer of the city—an evidence of how Christianity was now making its way even in the official classes. The modest little note by Tertius is of special interest. It was he who had written this letter, and no doubt the long one preceding it, to Paul's dictation, and had made copies of them so that we possess them now. He well deserved the honour of speaking for a moment in his own name. Another benediction brings the letter to a definite end, but is followed in our present text by a long and ornate doxology. This is made up in the main of quotations from Paul's writings, but is not at all in his manner. In some manuscripts, as we have seen, it appears at the end of the fourteenth chapter, and from others it is entirely absent. The probability is that it was added by a later hand when the note to Ephesus was incorporated in the Epistle to Romans, and the need was felt for something impressive that would round off the work as a whole. One cannot but feel that the great Epistle ends more fitly with the simple and heartfelt blessing, " The God of peace be with you all " (xv. 33) than with this wordy and pompous doxology.

III

THE CENTRAL TEACHING
OF THE EPISTLE

AFTER you have looked closely for some time at a great picture or building you stand back and consider it as a whole. The details have impressed and perhaps bewildered you, and you need to see how they are blended and how they are all subordinate to a large design. This comprehensive view is necessary for the right understanding of Paul's Epistle to the Romans. It is crowded with ideas which claim attention separately; the course of its argument is involved and is often broken by digressions. What impression does it make on us when we allow all its different parts to fall into harmony? Which of its many conceptions stand out from the others and give them significance? We have here an account of Christianity by one of its greatest teachers. What was its essential meaning for the mind of Paul?

As we thus stand back and contemplate the whole Epistle some issues which appeared to be all-important are seen to be secondary. For instance, Paul has much to say in this, as in his other letters, on the relation of the Law to the gospel. This was one of the most urgent questions which confronted the early church, and Paul was obliged to answer it, with the result that his Epistle has sometimes been taken as merely a counterblast to the current Judaistic teaching. When it is so read it appears to contain little that is of permanent value. As Christians we no longer feel bound to the Jewish Law, and have no need of Paul's laboured argument to convince us that faith in Christ is sufficient by itself. But Paul deals with the Law only by way of illustration. He sees in it the outstanding example of a mistaken type of religion which has now been superseded. So far from making

F

it the one object of his attack, he puts it on the same level with all the religions which men have vainly followed in the past. "There is no difference between the Jew and the Greek "; this is the point of view from which the whole Epistle is written. Men have been seeking God in the wrong way, and. the right one is now open to them. The Jews must no longer pride themselves on a unique privilege, for men of all races are on the same footing in the sight of God, and have fallen under the same condemnation. Paul is concerned with the Law only as it exemplifies the radical error in all the previous efforts to win favour with God. Over against it he sets the Christian message, and his one interest is in this new revelation of the truth.

There is another misunderstanding of Paul's intention which falls out of sight when the Epistle to Romans is considered as a whole. It is often called the great theological Epistle, and theologians in all ages have made it their happy hunting ground. Out of one chapter and another they have culled the doctrines which they have worked up into creeds and systems, so that it is associated in our minds with arid disputations of which most men have now grown weary. We ask, not unnaturally, whether it is not time to leave Paul's metaphysics alone and get back to the realities of the Christian message. Jesus stands before us in the Gospels as a living Person; Paul has changed Him into an imaginary figure, and replaced His clear demands with dogmas and speculations. But this is precisely what Paul has not done. His whole effort from first to last is to convince us that Christ lived on earth and did those things which we believe of Him. This sense of a historical fact is the very essence of what we call Paul's theology. Scholars have been at much pains in recent times to demonstrate, by a minute analysis, that in the thinking of Paul there is almost nothing that is definitely new. Quite literally he was debtor to Jews and Greeks and bar- barians. Trained as a Jewish Rabbi he thought out his Christian beliefs on the basis of Rabbinical teaching. A native of Tarsus, one of the centres of Greek learning, his mind had been steeped, almost unconsciously, in the Greek philosophical ideas. Travelling, as he did, over half-barbarous lands he was affected, more than he ever knew, with mystical conceptions which can be traced back to the old mythologies of the east. It can be shown that for almost every sentence he ever wrote some parallel can be found in the Jewish or Pagan literature of his time. He has no doubt brought the old ideas into new combinations and applied them in a Christian sense, but they did not originate with himself. Much has been made of this derivative strain in Paul's teaching, but it may be answered that there has never been a thinker yet who was not indebted in the same way to those who had gone before him. " I can see a little farther than other men," said Sir Isaac Newton, " because I stand on the shoulder of giants." This is the necessary condition of all thought, and of all true originality.

In Paul's theology, then, viewed merely from the intellectual side, there is little that is specifically new. You may take one of his doctrines after another and show that there was something like it in men's minds already, and that it has little to do intrinsically with the Christian revelation. Yet there was one thing in Paul's thinking that was tremendously new, and it was in this and not in any of his doctrines that his message consisted. He declared that what men had hitherto only dreamed of had now become real. God had manifested Himself in a life that had appeared on earth. Those ideals towards which the minds of men had been aspiring were no longer up in the clouds. They had come within reach and could be apprehended, just as surely as the things we touch and see. Paul describes his preaching by an expressive word (*Kerygma*), which means literally a proclamation made by a herald. He had been sent forth, like a messenger after a victorious battle, to announce something which had now been done. Men had been hoping and doubting and surmising, but all this was now over. The thing they had been waiting for was an accomplished fact.

Paul's message, therefore, is not to be sought in his

theology, which at most is only the wrapping of it. Nothing would have surprised him more than to learn that his doctrines, sometimes thrown out casually to meet an immediate difficulty, would one day be regarded as vital to the Christian faith. He would have said to-day, as he said in his lifetime to the Corinthians, " Who is Paul and who is Apollos but ministers through whom ye believed? " The word of the teacher had value only as it served to convince men of the truth he was seeking to proclaim. In whatever form he might present it he was intent only on this truth, and his hearers must try to perceive it behind the form. It is in this manner that we must read the Epistle to the Romans. Its real teaching is not to be found in the theological arguments, and when these only are considered we learn little of Paul's mind, whether we agree with him or not. If he had been writing to different people or in a different age he would doubtless have reasoned on other lines. His interest is not in the doctrines he puts forward but in the facts they are meant to explain. Christ had appeared on earth, and had died for man's salvation. This was Paul's message, and it meant everything to him. How could he bring it home to others? How could he awaken in them something of his own faith in Christ and in the wonderful thing which He had done? Unless the Epistle has so affected us we may have mastered all its theology and have yet missed the whole drift of its teaching.

One thing has always to be borne in mind, that Paul was not a secluded thinker but an active missionary, whose task it was to win converts for Christianity in the Gentile world. He wrote his letter to the Romans with this task in view. Rome was the gateway into a wider field than he had yet worked in. The church in this imperial city was symbolical to him of a future church which would spread itself over the whole world. Throughout the Epistle we are reminded at every turn of the universal scope of the gospel. By its very nature it is for all men and must be offered to all and will provide something for which all are seeking. No interpretation of the Epistle can be adequate which takes account only of special ideas and doctrines which are set forth in it. Paul's object is to get down to that ultimate message which makes Christianity a universal religion. What is the fundamental need which puts all men on the same level, whatever may be their race or standing? What is the truth in the gospel which constitutes its very substance and to which all men must respond? It is this which gives a unique and permanent value to the Roman Epistle. Confronted with a missionary task far bolder and more comprehensive than any he had yet undertaken, preparing to offer his message to people of whom he knew nothing except that they were men like himself, Paul rises above side-issues and considers what the gospel is in its essential nature, and why all mankind have need of it. This is the real theme of the Epistle.

When we look, then, not so much at his theological argument as at the convictions which underlie and inspire it, how does Paul conceive of the Christian message? His main contention is surely this—that God has now done for us what we have been vainly trying to do for ourselves. Everything else in the Epistle may be said to turn on this one idea. It is presented from different points of view and is enforced by reasoning and illustration, by experience and scriptural authority; but the one truth is always kept before us, and all others are viewed in the light of it. God has entered our world and has wrought a salvation which was utterly beyond the power of man. All that we have desired and imagined has been done for us, and we have only to accept this marvellous gift of God.

In order that we may apprehend this truth Paul sets himself, in the first place, to give us a right conception of God. He shows that men have erred in their past endeavours because they have failed to understand God's nature. They find themselves in a world where they get nothing unless they have worked for it, and it is not surprising that they should carry this principle into their religion. They want a great benefit from God, but take for granted that He will not give them

anything which they have not earned. Tolstoi has somewhere
described how he wished to brighten the lives of his peasants,
and presented them with a concert-hall and a playing-field,
all at his own expense. He wondered that they never availed
themselves of these benefits, but the reason was, as he
gradually discovered, that they suspected some deep-laid
scheme for over-reaching them. No one in his right mind
would ever give anything for nothing. This is the normal
attitude of worldly wisdom, and more than anything else it
has put a barrier between men and God. They think of Him
as reckoning His wages carefully in return for service done,
and of grudging them even what they have fairly earned.
The Jewish Law was based on this conception of God, and
the same may be said of all our ethical systems. More than
ever at the present day, when we have learned to explain
everything by mechanical law, we build our religion on this
basis. With the steward in the parable we liken God to an
austere man who exacts the strict price for everything he
bestows.

Paul is convinced that this is not the true nature of God.
He does not measure out to us just what we have worked for,
but gives freely according to His own boundless grace. A
generous man resents your unwillingness to take anything
from him which you cannot claim as your due. This is to
question the spirit in which he gives, to impute to him base
motives which were never in his mind. He gives because he
finds a pleasure in giving. All that he wants from you is your
gratitude, and if you are ungrateful he still gives. This, as
Paul had come to realize, is the nature of God. You may
gain some things by your own effort, but all your best possessions, and life itself with all that gladdens and enriches
it, have simply come to you. Nothing is asked of you but
to receive what has been given you by a bountiful unseen
hand. Paul cannot doubt that it must be the same with that
supreme blessing which all men desire. They feel themselves
in bondage and long for salvation. To find it has been the
one aim of all religions, but hitherto they have all missed the

way. It has been assumed that men must somehow win salvation for themselves. If they only performed certain difficult tasks, if they applied their minds and worked out some abstruse philosophy or moral code they would at last obtain what they sought so earnestly. These methods, however, have all failed, for they took no account of the nature of God. He is not a grudging taskmaster but the God of grace, and when He purposes any great good for men He gives it without their asking. By their insistence on doing everything themselves they push away the gift which needs only to be received. This, for Paul, is the meaning of the Christian message, and there is nothing in it that is strange and incredible when once we understand the nature of God. He gives everything to us freely, and now He has given us His salvation.

What is meant, then, by salvation? Paul does not conceive of it in terms of a future state of blessedness, as it is described in the book of Revelation. No doubt it is conjoined in his mind with the idea of immortality, but he thinks of it as given, essentially, in the present. The future will only bring more fully to light what is attainable in this life, although while burdened with the earthly body it cannot be fully realized. It is here and now that we must rise from the dead, for sin and death are inseparable, and while sin has the mastery of us we do not truly live. The true man, whom God has made in His own image, is buried as in a tomb, and when once he arises it is for ever. Death no more has dominion over him. He has come out into that higher life from which nothing can ever separate him.

Paul thus regards salvation under two aspects, a negative and a positive one. On the one hand we are saved out of the old state of existence, which he defines in general terms as one of sin. We are saved from it not merely in the sense that we now reform our evil habits of living, which a man may sometimes do by the force of his own will. Paul thinks rather of the whole constitution of man as at present corrupted. For all these ages men have been transgressing the

will of God, whether it was imposed on them by outward
law or written in their own hearts. Each new generation has
inherited the sin of all past ages and has added to it, and
the load has now become so terrible that all men feel helpless beneath it. In this idea of a sinfulness inherent in every
man's nature many have seen nothing but a crude superstition
which we have now outgrown, but Paul is only stating a fact,
capable almost of scientific proof. Each new person born
into the human race is involved from the very outset in all its
accumulated error. He carries a burden on his shoulders.
However noble his resolves may be he can do little, since
evil has become an element of the world he lives in, and of
his own mind and will. This is the rock on which all projects
of reform are sure to make shipwreck. There is evil in human
conditions because there is evil in man himself. He is born
to that inheritance of sin, transmitted to him age after age
from the beginnings of his life on earth.

Paul thinks, then, of salvation as the release from all that
weight of sin. Men are conscious of a bondage and imagine
that it is due to outward circumstance, or weakness of body,
or ignorance, or the malignity of other men. They keep
struggling in every way they can think of to break their
chains, but find themselves more and more entangled. For
the enemy that has enslaved them is nothing else than the
sin which has taken inward possession of them. They cannot
resist it because their will is helpless. They see what is right
but are compelled in spite of themselves to do what is wrong.
If they are ever to find deliverance it must be by a power
which is not their own, and this, for Paul, is the substance of
the Christian message. God has sent His Son into this
sinful world, and through Christ we have been set free.

Thus considered, salvation is the lifting of a burden, the
opening of a prison door, but, as Paul knows it, this release
from a previous state of misery is also the entrance into a
new one of joy and peace. Little is ever accomplished by
merely removing an evil thing. If there is not some positive
good to take its place a vacuum is left which is filled up by

and by with another evil. So it was not enough that men should be freed from sin. There needed to be a new energy which entered into them and worked in them for righteousness. In the same act whereby He saved them God had bestowed on them His life-giving Spirit. In their struggle with earthly passions and infirmities they were now aware of a power which helped them and enabled them to overcome. They were saved out of the old sinful life into a new and better one. In this region of Paul's thinking there is much that is difficult to explain, and perhaps he did not himself know how he should define the Spirit, and how it was related to God and to Christ and to the human soul. Yet he was certain of the fact that through faith in Christ a man was radically changed. He had found this true in his own experience. He had known countless men and women who in becoming Christians were possessed of a new kind of life. A higher nature had taken the place of the old one, and they were transformed at the very centre of their being. This, for Paul, was the mystery of the Christian life, as it has always been. He could only explain it from the entrance of a divine power, which worked in man's sinful nature and renewed it in the image of God.

Paul has thus shown how God Himself has accomplished for men what they could never do. They were conscious of a bondage, and had tried by methods of their own to win deliverance, but all their devices had failed. The more they struggled the more they realized their helplessness. God had now offered them as a free gift this salvation which they were vainly seeking. How can they avail themselves of the gift of God? This is the question which Paul sets himself to answer in the Epistle to Romans. He declares that salvation is by faith, and cannot be obtained in any other way.

From the beginning faith had been the watchword of Christianity. The name by which the earliest Christians had called themselves was " the believers ", that is, those who had faith that the promised Messiah had now appeared in Jesus of Nazareth. All that was necessary for baptism as a member of the church was a public confession of this belief. Yet the faith required was always something more than the mere assent to a given opinion. In accepting Jesus as Messiah you acknowledged that He had come from God, that He had a right over you as your Master, that your life must be ordered by His teaching. It is significant that from the first the confession required at baptism was not "Jesus is the Messiah" but "Jesus is Lord". The statement of belief was at the same time an oath of loyalty. Your faith involved the surrender of yourself to one whom you now regarded as your Lord.

Paul at his conversion had joined himself with the believers. He had confessed that Jesus, whose followers he had been persecuting, was indeed the Messiah, and he had undertaken henceforth to serve Him. But as time went on this act of belief had acquired an ever deeper meaning for Paul's mind. He had found that by owning Jesus to be the Messiah he had been led to a new conception of God, he had drawn closer to his fellow-men, he had become different in his own nature. All this had resulted from his act of belief and must somehow have been implied in it. So when he now spoke of faith he put into the word all that wealth of meaning which it now possessed for him. Believing in Christ you exchange your old life for a new one; you enter into a different relation to God and to men. What seemed to be only your assent to the Christian mode of belief was an act which affected your whole being, so much so that your faith carried with it your salvation.

It has been the misfortune of Paul that so many of the words he uses have come to be theological terms, which only a trained thinker can be expected to understand. Paul himself was not aware that his language was of this kind. He detested vague, high-sounding phrases, such as were employed by false teachers at Colossæ and elsewhere, and studied to express himself, not in a religious jargon, but in familiar words which would convey a sense of reality. So when he spoke of faith he did not wish to suggest anything mysterious. Everyone has known the condition of mind in which you forget yourself altogether, and allow some blessed influence to take entire possession of you. You look at a scene of nature, and the beauty of it sinks into you without your knowing. You mingle with a group of happy people, and your heart goes out to them in human kindness. The best moments of our lives are those in which we surrender ourselves wholly to some power which works in us of its own accord. As soon as we are recalled to some little personal interest the spell is broken, and that other power loses its hold. Paul takes this common experience and applies it to our relation to God. Here also is a power to which we must completely yield ourselves. God is seeking to give us something out of His fullness, and He cannot give it while we are busied with interests of our own. Those works by which we hope to earn salvation only shut us out from the power which alone can save us. Why not forget ourselves and open our hearts without reserve to God's love and goodness? This, in the last resort, is what Paul means by faith.

He thinks of faith, therefore, as that disposition in man which answers to the grace of God. The nature of God is to give freely; man's part is simply to receive, and without this willingness to receive he makes the grace ineffectual. In this sense we must understand that contrast of faith and works on which Paul is constantly insisting, and which has nothing to do, in its essence, with theological doctrine. It serves merely to emphasize the fact that man, in his self-importance, is for ever trying to do everything. Even in his common life he cannot rest from his fussy interference, and in this way misses the happiness which is waiting to come to him. In his religion likewise he cannot refrain from putting himself forward. He is convinced that unless he is always busy with some plan of his own contriving he cannot look for salvation. All the time he is only obstructing the action of God. It is God who must do everything, and all that He asks from man is to respond to Him, accepting what He desires to give. Salvation is by faith, and by faith alone. Instead of relying on their own poor effort men must throw themselves unreservedly on the grace of God.

Paul is well aware that to many people such teaching will appear dangerous. Does it not encourage a moral indolence? Might it not lead to the monstrous belief that the more we sin the more we may expect from God, whose goodness is most abundant when we have done least to deserve it? Paul's answer is that faith brings with it a new energy, and that this is its very purpose. A ship does not stand still when it spreads its sails to the winds of heaven; the power to which it yields itself is that which puts it in motion. The soul, likewise, when it surrenders to God is filled with the divine Spirit, which makes it capable, as it was not before, of all right action. Faith does not destroy the moral law, but enables us at last to fulfil the demands which have hitherto been beyond us. Paul shows how this had always been realized, in some measure, by earnest men. He was accused of preaching a novel doctrine when he maintained that faith was the life-blood of religion, but this was no discovery of his own. Long ago, before the Law existed, Abraham had simply believed God. It was in the might of this faith that he had conquered all weaknesses and become the father of a great nation. So Paul is confident that he re-asserts a principle which was clear to patriarchs and prophets, and which lies at the heart of all religion. The belief in God implies a conviction that all good things must come from God. Men have failed in their quest for salvation because they have not dared to take this conviction seriously. He calls on them to acknowledge what they know in their hearts to be true. Believing in God they must look to Him alone for salvation, and accept it as His gift.

The supreme act by which God has wrought our salvation is, for Paul, the death of Christ. By faith we respond to the grace of God, and His grace was manifested, once and for ever, in that sovereign act. "He who spared not his own Son, but gave him up for us all, will he not also with him freely give us all things?" His whole nature as the infinite Giver was summed up in the one gift. It has often been objected that Paul's thought of Christ is centred entirely in the single fact of His death on the Cross. He says almost nothing of His life and teaching. He had determined, as he tells us in 1 Corinthians, to think of nothing but of Christ crucified. It must be admitted that by thus restricting himself he leaves out much that would have broadened and illuminated his message, and as we read his Epistles we need continually to supplement them from our knowledge of the Gospels. Yet it is not true that he takes the death of Christ as an isolated fact, for which the life that had preceded it only forms a sort of pedestal. The death, as he conceives of it, was the life in its final outcome. It gathered up in one burning focus all that Jesus had taught and all His works of power and mercy. So, in his presentation of Christ, Paul takes Him at the grand revealing moment. You have only to behold Him as He was then if you would understand what He was, and how He fulfilled God's purpose.

Thus, in the death of Christ, Paul saw the divine act which effected our salvation. Men were seeking vainly to deliver themselves when God came to their rescue, and all that He requires of us is our faith, our acceptance of what He has Himself done. Paul's task as an Apostle was to proclaim the glorious thing which had actually happened on earth. God, who alone could do it, had wrought our salvation. Not only does Paul impress on us that Christ had died, but he tries to explain why the death had a redeeming value. He works with a theory suggested by the procedure of a law-court. All men as sinners were liable to condemnation, but, although they had no plea to offer, the divine Judge acquitted them on the ground of their faith. He accepts the suffering of Christ as compensation for all the evil they have done, and thus pronounces them just. On this side of his thought Paul is undoubtedly wrestling with a stern fact, which many who question his doctrine have too lightly overlooked. God is righteous and has founded His world on righteousness, and if He remitted the deadly consequences of sin He would be false to Himself. How can His grace be reconciled with His eternal justice? This is a tremendous problem, and Paul refuses to shut his eyes to it. Yet we cannot but feel that his answer is unsatisfying. The ways of God are not to be interpreted by any analogy of a human law-court, and by elaborating this idea Paul has obscured and complicated his message.

The truth is that we must distinguish between Paul's faith in the death of Christ and his doctrine of the Atonement. This particular doctrine is only one of a number by which he tries, in his various Epistles, to explain the mystery of why Christ died. In the Roman Epistle he gives it a special prominence, and perhaps it represents the conviction at which he finally arrived. Christ had taken on Himself the condemnation which had been incurred by the human race; in His own sufferings He had borne the penalty of sin, so that all men henceforth were free. There is much in the doctrine which is difficult, and to which we may rightly take exception, but Paul does not offer it as the ultimate truth. It is only his attempt to interpret a divine fact, and he wants us to believe the fact and not the interpretation. When men were helpless God intervened to help them. At a given place and time he manifested His love to us in the Cross of Christ. Paul's whole endeavour is to convince us of the actuality of this redeeming love. However we may explain the death of Christ, and to the end it will always remain a mystery, we can be sure of the fact, and on this we may rest our faith. Millions of men and women have found peace in Paul's conception of the great Atonement once made for them, but it is not the doctrine itself which moves and uplifts them. Few of them, probably, could give any clear account of what it means. What they respond to, in the very depth of their being, is the simple fact that Christ died for them. The love of God is no fond imagination, but expressed itself in a sublime act. This is the real message of Paul, and he tries to add to its significance by his impressive doctrine of why the death of Christ had such a redeeming power. We may not be satisfied with his doctrine, but his true aim in the Epistle to Romans is to make us realize the fact that Christ died on our behalf. We can trust in the love of God because He did this for us when we were yet sinners.

It is by faith that the meaning of the Cross is apprehended, and faith is the answer of each individual soul to the call of God. In much of his argument Paul appears to think in universal terms. All men sinned in Adam; mankind in the mass lies under bondage; Christ took upon Him the entire human burden; He died for the race of men, so that through Him all might be made alive. At times Paul seems almost to forget the separateness of human beings and to think only of a single humanity which has been subjected to sin and now has been set free. Jewish thinkers had regarded Israel as an indissoluble whole, a chosen race of which all the members had their portion in the favour of God. Paul might seem to adopt this Jewish conception, with the difference that he puts all mankind in place of the one people. Yet we can see, as we look deeper, that he has completely broken with this communal mode of thinking, which was that of ancient religion generally. Each nation had its own divinity who was supposed to watch over it, and the duty of individuals was to preserve their unity with the nation and so share in the common privilege. Paul had ceased to think in this manner. He believes that while the gift of God is offered to all, each man must decide for himself whether he will accept it. The appeal in Romans depends throughout on this conviction that every human being is a person, with his own individual place in the mind of God.

It is at this point that the idea of faith as the one way of salvation involved a radical change in all religious ideas. A man's religion had formerly been little more than one of his civic obligations. As he obeyed the laws of the state and took part in its defence, so he was bound to its religion. " Socrates does not worship the gods whom the city worships "; so ran the famous indictment, and it meant to the ancient mind that Socrates was at once a bad citizen and an impious man. The same idea that religion and country must go together lasted on into Christian times, and we have not yet escaped from it; but in principle it fell to the ground with the coming of Christianity. Here was a religion which had faith as its motive, and there can be no faith which is not personal. A man must

believe in God for himself; he must respond to God with that
which is deepest in his own soul. Paul describes the conflict
within a man when he wishes to do right but is constrained by
his lower nature to do wrong. This, he implies, is the struggle
of the true personality to assert itself. When you say " I "
and " me " you think of that man in you who, if he only could,
would be on the side of God. This is yourself, and it is to you,
in your inward personal being, that the Christian message is
addressed. God offers His salvation, not to the race or community of which you are a member, but to you as an individual
soul, and you must answer Him with a faith which is your own.

Paul seeks to affirm this more emphatically in that doctrine
of predestination which bulks so largely in the Epistle to
Romans. Considered merely as a doctrine it is beset with
many difficulties, and Paul perceives them clearly, and tries,
not very successfully, to answer them. But it is not hard to
see the essential idea which lies at the heart of the doctrine.
The individual man, as Paul regards him, is no mere chance
variation of a common type. He is a person, with his roots
in eternity. Before ever he was born or had done good or evil,
he existed as a person in the mind of God, who singled him
out and ordained his character and destiny. Paul's doctrine
has often been distorted into shapes which he never intended,
but under all these perversions it has served at least to impress
on men that they were individual souls. There can be no
hiding of themselves in the crowd, for God deals with them,
not in the mass, but as separate men and women. " Every one
of us must give account of himself unto God." It is in such a
verse as this that we must look for the central meaning of
Paul's idea. By his belief that God has predestined men, one
by one, he makes his grand affirmation of the worth of the
individual man. Christ died for the human race, but the gift
He brought was for each particular man. The faith by which
every man receives it must be his own, and cannot avail him
if it is only that of others. This reverence for the human
person, however obscure and neglected he may be, is an
essential element in the religion of Paul.

The regard for men as individuals has its outcome in that passion for liberty which breaks out ever and again in Paul's Epistles. His one theme in Romans is the deliverance which God has secured for us by His work of grace. We are set free from everything that has fettered us, and our faith is at the same time our assurance of perfect liberty, for in the act of faith a man reaches out to God, and is made aware that he belongs to God and to Him alone. This sense of freedom in the soul is the condition and the active principle of all freedom. Knowing that you are someone in your own right, and that God Himself has called you and sets a value on you, you can stand up against your fellow-men and against all the forces of this world. Henceforth you are God's man, and to your own Master you stand or fall.

It is with this inward freedom that Paul is chiefly concerned throughout the Epistle. Men have been enslaved by sin, and are now released. They have come out into a new life, and through Christ have attained to the glorious liberty of the children of God. But Paul proceeds to show how the spiritual freedom must determine the Christian attitude in all civic and social relations. The fourteenth chapter of Romans is one of the great land-marks in the history of liberty. It turns on what may appear a very trivial issue—the dissension of two parties in the Roman church, each of which was intent on imposing its practices on the other. But Paul takes this occasion to consider the whole question of freedom, in the light of the religious principles which he has set forth in the earlier chapters. He declares that a man's faith is personal to himself, and that when you have surrendered your life to God you are responsible only to God. You must obey your own conscience, which is the voice of God within you, and although it directs you in a path diverging from that of others you must still follow it. At all times you must do what you feel in your heart to be the will of God, and if you act otherwise you are false to Him and to yourself. And this liberty which you claim for yourself you must allow to other men. They also are accountable to God and must seek in their own way to do

G

His will. It is not for you or any man to stand between them and their true Master. Every man is a free personality in the service of God, and is therefore independent of the will of others. His one care must be to be faithful, in great things and small, to his own inner sense of what God commands him.

It appears strange at first sight that in these very chapters in which he proclaims his principle of freedom Paul makes his plea for obedience and mutual service. He warns his readers that they must submit to civil authority, which is ordained by God for the maintenance of order and justice. They must likewise work harmoniously together as members of the church. Each one must lay aside all personal interests and look only to the common welfare of the brethren. All this may seem to be quite contrary to the idea of individual liberty. We are told, almost in the same breath, that as Christians we are absolutely free, and that we must be content to give up our freedom. But there is no inconsistency. Liberty consists in obedience to Christ, the one Master, and we obey Him by serving one another. We do willingly for His sake what we once did under compulsion, and it is in this manner that we assert our liberty. By pure religious insight, Paul has grasped the principle on which, as the world is now learning, a free society must be built. Men are personal beings, and if they are to live in concord it must be of their own free will. So long as they are forced to co-operate, by however skilful an organization, they are all in discord, and are ready at any moment to spring apart. It is only free men who are able when necessary to resign their freedom, and to form a real community in which the good of each separate person is the good of all.

We have here the true answer to the common objection to Paul's teaching, especially as set forth in the Roman Epistle. It is argued that his religion is entirely self-centred. All that seems to matter to him is the saving of one's own soul. By an act of personal faith you are to make sure that you at least are set free, by the grace of God, from that condition of sinfulness into which mankind has fallen. Bunyan has described his pilgrim as escaping, with his burden still upon him, from the City of Destruction. All that he thinks of is to be released of his burden. He refuses even to look back on the city, for his one anxiety is not to share its doom. This, we are told, was Paul's religion, and it does not truly represent the gospel. Ought not the pilgrim, if he was worthy of his name of Christian, to have remained in the city and tried to save it from the threatened destruction? To make sure of your own safety is not enough. You are one with your fellow-men, and you cannot yourself be saved unless they are saved along with you. We sometimes boast of this social Christianity as our modern advance on the religion of Paul, but he never thought of neglecting it. He wrote this Epistle for the very purpose of awakening the Romans to a sense of their social duty. They had themselves learned the way of salvation, and the task was thus laid on them of making it known to others. This was the conviction of Paul, and also, it may be said, of Bunyan.

Our mistake in reading the Epistle is to leave out of sight the closing chapters, which deal entirely with practical obligations. They seem to have no connection with the theological argument which has gone before, but they are integral to it, and it cannot be properly understood apart from them. Paul is, indeed, concerned with the individual soul, for each man must hear the call of God for himself and answer it with his personal faith. But what is true of one man is true of all. When you are made aware of your own deepest needs you are brought into sympathy with other men, whom you have hitherto regarded as strangers. You understand now what they are seeking; you are filled with the desire to help them. Thus the account of what the gospel is, in its essential nature, merges naturally in the later enquiry into its larger implications. The Christian seeks his own salvation, but in doing so he becomes a member of the Christian society. He grows alive to his duties as a citizen, and a brother in the family of mankind. This, it is hardly too much to say, is the inner motive of the whole Epistle. Paul seeks to lift us out of our narrow and selfish lives and unite us in all our sympathies with our fellow-men. This he does by bringing us to a deeper knowledge of our own souls, and of what God has done for us through Christ.

For many centuries the Epistle to Romans was accepted without question as the grand manifesto of our religion. Creeds and catechisms were all based on it. The doctrines laid down in it were the authoritative statements of all Christian truth. To many people this estimate of it has now grown more than doubtful. As they pass from the Gospels to this Epistle they feel that much is wanting, and that much is added which belongs more to metaphysical theory than to the teaching of Jesus. They hold that even when the thought is truly Christian it is presented in forms which are quite foreign to the simplicity of the Christian message. It is thus concluded that this Epistle, instead of explaining our religion, has obscured and in some measure perverted it. The time has now arrived when we should forget all the laboured argument of Romans and find our way back to some more vital conception of the Christian faith.

In this judgment of the Epistle we impute to Paul a false assumption which is really our own, and which he did not share. Christianity, as we conceive it, is a system of beliefs which can be definitely stated. Paul was a man of the first century, who thought and spoke in the manner of his time. We belong to a different world, and many of his ideas are no longer valid. We desire a new statement of the gospel, more in keeping with the thought of our own day. But the truth is that Christianity cannot be defined in any doctrines, either in those of Paul or in any others we may put in their place. This was fully apparent to Paul himself. When he tries to describe what it is that makes a Christian he can only say " we have the mind of Christ ", " we have the Spirit ", " we walk by faith and not by sight ". He never intended his doctrines to be the final expressions of Christian truth. By means of them he only sought to make intelligible, in some degree, to the reason what must be apprehended in another way. In reading the Epistle to Romans we must never forget that it culminates in the glorious eighth chapter, in which Paul throws aside his argument and declares triumphantly what Christ has done for him. It is not by any reasoning but by this living experience that he has learned the meaning of the gospel.

In its central teaching, therefore, the Epistle is not theological. Paul's object in writing it is not so much to formulate and prove his opinions as to communicate something of the invincible faith which possessed him. " I know," he says, at the close of his letter, " that you are well able to instruct one another, but I have written, without any reserve, only to put you in remembrance." This is no mock humility. He is aware after he has done his best that he has thrown little new light on the Christian message. He will be well content if he has induced his readers to look back on their own lives and consider how the faith in Christ has transformed them. Paul never attached much value to his theories for their own sake. They corresponded with his own thinking, but another teacher, Apollos or Cephas or someone else, would think differently. Each of them, in his own manner, would point the way to the truth, but they would all be far short of it. " We have this treasure," he confessed, " in earthen vessels." The vehicle was frail and temporary at the best, but it served, with all its imperfection, to convey the treasure. This is the only value of any theology that can ever be devised, and we must fix our minds not on the vessel, but on that which it contains. Paul framed his doctrines out of the materials which lay to his hands, and many of his arguments appear to our minds outworn and unconvincing. Yet his Epistle is still, as in times past, one of the priceless possessions of the Christian world. More than any other book it brings home to us the abiding principles of our religion. The vessel may be inadequate, but assuredly it contains the treasure.

We learn from it that men in themselves are helpless. They have fallen into a bondage from which they struggle to get free, but their own efforts are futile and must ever be so. That which they cannot do God has Himself done for them. His nature is to give, out of His own free goodness, and in Christ

He has offered us His salvation. Nothing is required of us but faith on our part to receive what God has given. Faith is the one means of deliverance, and it also carries with it a divine power which renews the nature of men, and supports them in all right action, and brings them into true fellowship with one another. The Epistle to the Romans is not the final statement of Christianity, for there can never be one. But it insists with a matchless power on the fundamental Christian beliefs, and we must always go back to it for new insight and inspiration.

IV

THE VALUE OF THE
EPISTLE TO-DAY

PAUL has told us, in a memorable passage, of the dangers that had beset him in his work for the gospel. "Thrice was I beaten with rods, once was I stoned, thrice I suffered shipwreck, a night and a day I have been on the deep." These stormy experiences of his lifetime have pursued him after his death. Ever and again the church has turned violently against him. He has been beaten and stoned and shipwrecked, but through it all he has survived. In the end the church has always come back to Paul, and the return to him has been the beginning of a religious advance. Augustine and Anselm, Luther, Wesley, the evangelists of last century took up the Pauline ideas when they seemed to be discarded, and by means of them put new vigour into the Christian cause. This vitality of Paul cannot be due to any accident. If he had stood only for some old-world form of belief he would long ago have been swept aside by the new currents of religious thought. He has held his own in virtue of an abiding truth in his message. Men have continued to feel that he had laid hold of essential things, and that the gospel he proclaimed was still the power of God.

There are clear signs in our own day of a return to Paul, but the movement for a long time past has been away from him. For a night and a day he has been on the deep. We constantly hear it said that the modern world, if it is to endure, must have some form of Christianity, but it must not be the dogmatic religion of the Epistle to Romans. This, in a sense, may be true. Our age is different from that of Paul or Augustine or Luther, and even from that of our fathers. Ideas which they took for granted have now grown questionable, and we cannot express our beliefs in just the old language. Paul himself, if he had been living now, would not have reasoned in the manner he does in Romans. Nevertheless, by processes of thought which are not ours, he arrives at principles which belong to the substance of our religion. They must be valid for Christians to-day no less than for those Roman Christians to whom he wrote. It may even be claimed for them that the lapse of time has served only to establish them, and that they have more meaning now than they had at first.

If we have travelled far since the Epistle was written, our journey, in some respects, has been in a circle, and we have come round to an age which is curiously similar to that of Paul. There is much in his thought which is far more intelligible now than in any previous generation. In that first century the world had broken with the past, and was feeling vaguely towards a new order. The various races were fusing together in the great Roman Empire; a common culture was forming itself; old loyalties had lost their hold, and moral sanctions were weakening along with them. It was not a creative age, but was intensely critical. Things that had been accepted as a matter of course were put to the question and found wanting, with the result that the general attitude was one of scepticism. There seemed no longer to be any truth on which men could depend, and they fell back on superstitions, or gave an eager welcome to every novel theory. As we read the classical literature of the first and second centuries we almost forget that it comes to us from a remote time. The attitude of mind which it reflects is very much our own. The interests with which it deals are those which occupy us at the present day. We can understand those men of the Roman world far better than we know our own countrymen of a few generations ago, because their outlook on life was so much more similar to ours. They possessed what we now call the modern mind.

Paul wrote his Epistle for people who lived at the very centre of that old civilization. He was himself a Roman citizen, and was affected more than he knew by the prevailing influences. In his opening chapter he draws a lurid picture of the world he lived in, but we can see, from many indications in his writings, that he was proud of it. Men had room in that vast well-ordered empire to move freely. Their minds also were free to wander over all the fields of knowledge. As he launches out, as he delights to do, into far-reaching speculations, Paul could not but remind himself that in earlier days this would have been impossible. The mental horizon was then a narrow one, while he was privileged to live in this new time, when all prospects had widened. As we see him now, Paul was a man of antiquity, limited in all his thinking by the conditions of his time. We need to remember that he did not regard himself in this manner. He never doubted that he belonged to an enlightened age in which almost everything that could be learned by human wisdom was fully known. He writes to the Romans as a modern man, whose readers also were in sympathy with the new time.

It is his pride in the age he lives in which gives weight to the charges he brings against it. He admits that in point of knowledge men have gone forward, but declares that their wisdom, pursued for its own sake, has been their calamity. They have grown self-sufficient, and have ceased to feel the need of God or to take Him into account. The consequence has been that they have lost all sense of reality. They mistake evil for good, and base things for noble, and while they never doubt that they are progressing they have been falling steadily backward. In this analysis of the first century culture there is much that applies, with almost startling accuracy, to our own. We also have been proud of our wisdom, and in our reliance on it have become fools. Nations that seemed to be leading in the march of knowledge have plunged back, to the world's amazement, into utter savagery. They have been guilty, deliberately, of deeds so vile and horrible that it is sickening even to think of them. All this, as Paul perceived when he looked at the corruptions of his own day, has been only the natural outcome of knowledge worshipped for itself. Men had grown confident that the human mind could prescribe its own laws and purposes. They refused to acknowledge God in their thoughts, and became vain in their imaginations. They set earthly things in the place of God—power, the state, material wealth and comfort—and in their idolatry of these things sank lower and lower until they became as beasts. The war has been a judgment in the sense that it has brought home to us, in a manner there can be no mistaking, the deadly error of trusting wholly in the wisdom of men. With our own eyes we have seen the wrath of God revealed from heaven against all unrighteousness and ungodliness. If the highest is not honoured as the highest, if the creature is put before the Creator, everything becomes false and will some day crash into ruin. When the tower of Siloam fell this did not prove that all who were buried beneath it were grievous sinners; the judgments of God are not to be interpreted in that manner. But it did prove that there was something wrong with the construction of the tower. The law of gravity cannot be mocked, and walls that are not built squarely on sound foundations are certain to fall. A similar law holds good in the moral order. There must first be the right relation to God, and when this is wanting men will only labour to their own confusion.

The parallel of our time to that of Paul may be carried further. Living as we do, under like conditions, we have come round, in our ordinary thinking, to some of the ideas which underlie his Epistle. He maintains, for one thing, that humanity must be considered as a single whole. However men have divided themselves into races and classes they are all of the same flesh and blood, and have fallen into the same errors, and if ever they are saved they must be saved together. As a citizen of the one great empire Paul has been forced to this conviction, and he develops it in its religious significance. On this side of his thought we are now in sympathy with him as no previous age could be. Distances have been narrowed, and the interests of all peoples are closely interwoven. The differences which were formerly so all-important are counting for less and less, and a time is in sight when they will disappear. Already we are learning to examine all questions in their bearing on the whole family of mankind.

Again, Paul has that historical sense which we sometimes think of as peculiar to the modern mind. He is aware that all events are mysteriously linked together, that the present must be understood in its relation to the great human drama which has been unfolding itself ever since time began. Paul's philosophy of history is indeed very different from ours. Instead of an unbroken progress from the lower to the higher he sees a continual deterioration. Men were made in the image of God, but sin entered in and they were estranged from Him, and as time went on they wandered even farther astray until they were utterly lost. It may be that Paul was wrong in his reading of history, though we must not claim too positively that we are right. However this may be, he has grasped the idea of a continuity, of an inner coherence in the life of the human race. He is always seeking to explain present conditions in view of what has happened in past ages, and it is from this historical side that we now approach all problems.

Again, he is profoundly conscious that man is in bondage. We have aspirations to which we can never attain. We know what is right, but are compelled by forces too strong for us to do what is wrong. We feel that we were made for freedom, but at every point find ourselves in chains. For Paul, the power which overmasters us is that of sin; for modern thought it is the material environment in which we must pursue our moral and intellectual life. But, however we try to account for it, the prevailing mood in our time is one of frustration. The present century began with a great wave of optimism. Man had accomplished so much that there seemed to be no limit to his capacity, and to the well-being in store for him. Since then he has done more wonderful things than ever, but his hopes have ended in disappointment. There is a growing sense that life is nothing but a deception. Do what we will, the powers which oppress us will never lose their hold, and at best we can only change one form of misery for another. Millions of people are repeating in their countless different ways Paul's cry of despair; " O wretched man that I am: who will deliver me from this body of death."

Again, it may be claimed for our generation that we are in sympathy with that passion for righteousness which inspires the Epistle to Romans. Not so long ago the whole emphasis in Christian teaching was on the divine love and forgiveness. It was felt that Paul had misinterpreted the gospel. Assured though he was of the ultimate mercy of God, he yet clung to the old conception of Him as the inflexible Judge who could not but inflict punishment on the evil-doer. Paul, it was maintained, had never really entered into the true spirit of Christianity, which proclaims the infinite goodness of God. Our human laws demand a strict justice; God forgives without condition or reserve, and as Christians we must act as God Himself does. We have been rudely shaken out of this one-sided attitude by the terrible events of recent years. It has been impressed on us that justice is the necessary foundation of everything. God must uphold it, and men must co-operate with God. Forgiveness has no meaning unless we first believe in justice and make certain that it is done on earth. So we are now willing to recognize that it was not Paul, but ourselves, who misunderstood the nature of Christianity. It magnifies the love of God, but its primary message is still that of the Hebrew prophets that He is the righteous God, who will in no wise clear the guilty. There may be much in Paul's teaching with which we disagree, but he speaks for ourselves when he asserts the fundamental fact of the justice of God.

Paul wrote, then, in a period of the world's history which was strangely like our own, more like it than any other which has come between. His Epistle is not to be read as an abstract theological document. It was written in view of the actual conditions in which the first readers found themselves, and has a definite message to ourselves, who live under similar conditions. Paul takes our present difficulties and shows us that there is one way, and only one, by which they can be overcome. When we thus read the Epistle as intended, in a manner, for our own time, what does it teach us of some great truths which, in our modern religion, have been too much forgotten?

In the first place it impresses on us, with tremendous power, the reality of sin. This word, it has often been remarked, has largely disappeared from our religious language. Our emphasis is all on the natural goodness of man and the need for developing it and guiding it wisely. In so far as there is evil in human nature it is set down to some deficiency for which, in most cases, we cannot be held responsible. The man whom we call wicked was born with a flaw in mind or body; he received, perhaps in early childhood, a moral injury from which he never recovered; he was placed in wrong surroundings, or was pursued by evil fortune. For that part, it is often pointed out that a vice may be nothing but a virtue which has never found its proper outlet. The criminal, if only his energy had been turned in another direction, might have stood out as a saint or a hero. All this is true, and it is well that we are learning to pass fairer judgment on human weaknesses which in former times were classed indiscriminately as sin. Paul himself pleads for this justice. He reminds us that we are not to single out one man from another as sinful, for all have sinned, and fallen short of the glory of God. Men as men are under a bondage, and with their inner will are on the side of good, although they are powerless to put their will into action. Yet he insists that this does not alter the fact and the dreadfulness of sin. When you do wrong you may find many excuses for it; you may argue that all men act as you do; you may blame your conduct on your parentage, or your circumstances, or the society you live in; but all the time you know that it is wrong. Whatever may be the cause you have broken the law of God written in your heart, and before God you stand condemned. We take it as the very mark of an honest man that he accepts the responsibility for his error, and does not try to push it over on someone else; and this must also be our attitude before God. Until we acknowledge our personal sinfulness we pretend to be what we are not, and can neither ask nor receive anything at His hands. Attempts have been made to cure disease by simply refusing to admit that it is there, and this method has been adopted, in much of our modern religion, with regard to sin. But the malady which you will not confess is still eating its way and gradually destroying you; and it is not otherwise with the sin.

It is nothing else than this refusal to own man's sinfulness which defeats our effort to better the world's condition. Social service, for many people in our time, has largely taken the place of religion, and no one can deny that those who fight the battle against poverty and ignorance and injustice are doing the work of God. By whatever name they choose to call themselves they are Christ's disciples. But it is their tragedy that their best endeavours for the most part prove futile. After all that has been done to diffuse knowledge and humanize industry and raise all the standards of living to a higher level there are few signs of a better society. Often it would appear as if all endeavour to improve the world leads only to some increase in its misery. The reason is that we leave out of account the primary fact that men are sinful. There is an evil in their nature which is not removed by anything we can devise to help them, and which only asserts itself more vigorously when it is given more room to work in. It is idle to persuade yourself that men are wicked because they are ill-paid and badly governed. The trouble lies much deeper. It is inherent in the nature of men, and when this is denied or forgotten the best effort is thrown away. And as it is with the people you work for, so is it with yourself. You are not a man naturally good, who lapses now and then into errors which can be easily corrected. That is how most of us think of ourselves, and it is for this reason that we never grow any better. Sin is an element of our very being, and infects everything we think and do. How is it to be uprooted?

Paul is occupied throughout the Epistle to Romans with this fact of sin. We are not to think of him as teaching an antiquated theology which we can now afford to leave behind us. He looks courageously at a grim fact of our human life, which is the same now as when he wrote. We have tried too much to conceal it from ourselves, and that is one reason why we stand in urgent need of Paul's message. It brings us face to face with the truth that man, with all his splendid possibilities, is sinful, and we must reckon with that truth before we can do anything. The first thing necessary when you commit yourself to any enterprise is to know the chief obstacle that has to be overcome. If you shut your eyes to it, or try to minimize it, you play the fool and are sure to meet with disaster. Paul makes it plain that the great obstacle in the path of all men is the evil in their own hearts. They must not hide from themselves that it is there. They must try to discover some means of removing it, or all their struggle will be in vain.

Man is in bondage, and his deliverance must come from God. Of himself he can do nothing, and he must stand aside and allow God to work for him. If he trusts in his own effort he obstructs the action of God and loses what would have come to him as a free gift. The Epistle to Romans turns on this idea, and it is just here that the modern mind has most violently broken away from Paul. As a result of all the advances made in the last century we have unlimited confidence in what man himself can do. We are never tired of reminding ourselves that in past ages, the so-called ages of faith, men waited passively on God, expecting that He would act for them. He did nothing, and now they have ventured to act on their own behalf, and the things they waited for have been accomplished. They have at last perceived the right method. Instead of looking to some invisible power above them they must take the management of the world into their own hands. They have capacities in their nature which previously they never dreamed of, and nothing is necessary but to put forth their energy and work and plan for themselves. The religion of the future, we are often told, is this faith in humanity. Paul spoke for a bygone age when men were ignorant of their powers and afraid to use them. Now we are discovering what men can do, and we must put our trust in this new revelation.

We are reminded in the Epistle to Romans that the same mood prevailed in the ancient world. Men were living in an age of enlightenment and had put the past behind them.

They never doubted that by their own wisdom they could find the way of deliverance. The result, as Paul could see, had been far otherwise. There had never been a time when evil in every form had been so rampant. Beneath all the show of a splendid civilization the world was going to pieces. Thoughtful men are beginning to wonder whether the same process is not repeating itself in our own time. It was hardly questioned fifty years ago that a great new age was now opening, but it seems further away than ever. Horrors which appeared to be finally banished from human society—slavery and despotism, vile superstitions, famine and torture and persecution—have all come back. The road which we followed so trustfully had been leading all the time to a precipice, and now, as we start again, the future is utterly dark. Our minds are full of new schemes and devices, but no one any longer has much confidence in them. They are the same in kind as those which have been tried already and have failed. Can we believe that it will be any different now?

The message of Paul has thus a meaning to us which it could not have, even a few years ago. He tells us that with all our effort we can do very little, and that we must put our trust in a higher power which will bestow on us as a gift what we can never effect ourselves. Paul is thinking of the supreme gift of salvation, but his principle holds good of almost everything that is worth having. By insisting that we must do the whole work ourselves we miss the divine gift. One thinks, for instance, of that new social order on which our hopes are centred. From the time of Plato onward schemes have been put forward for breaking up our present society and reconstructing it on an entirely new pattern. It is assumed that man by his own intelligence can work out a system in which all human relations will be different, and the social interests will fit into each other as in a well-oiled machine. No doubt there is need for much readjustment, but it is always dangerous to play with life and overdo our planning. Men are so made that they live in families, that they are drawn together by mutual needs and affections, that they vary in character and aim and capacity, and they discover, without knowing how, the kind of society which suits them best. A power outside of our own will and ingenuity keeps moulding all our arrangements, and we must be content to work along with it. By too much interference we only defeat the higher will which is wiser than we are, and which will do for us in natural course what we could never do.

In the individual life, likewise, we do not secure happiness and peace of mind by our own planning. No one, as a rule, is so miserable as the man who deliberately sets out to be happy, and directs all his habits and activities to this one end. Happiness comes to the child, who does not know that he has it; it comes to the good workman and the unselfish friend, to the lover and the parent and the bold adventurer, who are bent on quite other aims. If you are ever to have it you must take it as an unsought gift, and so it is with all the best things in life. They are given to us by an unseen hand, and when we plan for them too carefully they pass us by.

This is the truth which in our time we are in danger of forgetting. We have made up our minds that nothing can ever be accomplished unless we do it, of set purpose, for ourselves. This we acclaim as our great discovery—that we must make our lives by methods of our own devising, while men supposed in former days that if they did their little part honestly their lives would somehow be made for them. Perhaps they were too trustful, but we have fallen into a much more dangerous error. Always intent on what we can do ourselves we have lost sight of the greater power which works on our behalf. We complain that God has forgotten us while it is we who keep pushing ourselves forward and getting in His way. He did not place men here as in a solitude, where nothing was provided for them and they had to make everything themselves. He surrounded them on every hand with His bounty; He furnished them with deep instincts on which they could rely when their little store of wisdom failed them. In his Roman Epistle Paul proclaims

H

this message of the grace of God, and it is a many-sided and far-reaching one, which we need more than any other in this anxious time.

He declares therefore that in our religion, as in all else, we must look not to our own righteousness but to God's free gift. We are justified by faith and not by works. There was a time when this pronouncement of Paul brought with it a revelation. It came to Luther, and when its meaning dawned upon him he felt much as Columbus had done a few years before when he first looked out on the new world. The magic has now gone out of it. We associate it with arid controversies, and with a type of religion which has little appeal to the modern mind. We still look for a Kingdom of God, but are persuaded that we ourselves must bring it in. Our trust is in our own righteousness—in the efficacy of our social and political reforms, our scientific achievement, our improvements in all the machinery of well-being. This we call practical religion, and we dismiss all other as antiquated and visionary.

Now it is just this attitude of mind which Paul is thinking of when he declares that men are justified by faith. He would have us see that we can do little by our own endeavour, and must allow the higher power to work for us. At the same time he makes it clear that while faith consists in waiting on God it is also the true source of energy. A man soon discovers the limits of his own strength. Aiming at a distant goal he finds that after he has done his utmost he has made only a few yards of progress, and if he were left to himself he would give up in despair. But he knows of a power which works along with him, and will support him through failure and discouragement, and make something great out of his own small effort. As Paul looks back on the mission which had proved so wonderfully fruitful he acknowledges that he can claim no credit of his own. He knows that he has been sustained, through all these laborious years, by his faith in God, and if he has achieved anything it is only because God has used him as His instrument. It is safe to say that every man who has ever succeeded in a high task would make the same confession. "Not having my own righteousness but the righteousness which is of God by faith." Paul expresses himself in theological language, but these words of his might stand as the motto of every victorious life.

This, then, is the element which we need to recover in our modern religion. It is often complained that religion is now in a state of decay, but this is not true. Perhaps in future histories our age will be singled out as one of religious revival. It will be shown that in this twentieth century men took the Christian principles and applied them, almost for the first time, to social institutions, to the intercourse of nations, to matters of industry and business and the whole conduct of life. This, in the highest sense, is religious progress, and we have a right to be proud of it. Our modern saints may look very different from those in the stained-glass windows, but in their labour for justice, for the relief of poverty, for better understanding between races, they are just as truly the disciples of Christ. Our religion has not decayed because it is more intent on action than on doctrine or mystical contemplation. One thing, however, is too often wanting in it, and that is the conviction that God is behind our action. We want to see plainly where we are going; we take careful measure of our abilities, and hold ourselves excused when even an obvious duty appears too hard for us. It is this, more than anything else, which discredits our religion in the eyes of the world. The question is asked, and is sometimes very difficult to answer, "What do ye more than others?" Is there anything in the Christian rule of life, as it is usually practised, which is not well within the reach of common prudential morality? It is evident, even to those outside of the church, that Christianity calls for deeds and sacrifices which are beyond the ordinary man. It gives the assurance that those who believe in God have God Himself to rely on, and will venture where other men draw back. The diver, fathoms deep in the ocean, springs up to a rock which rises high above his head. He knows that he is moving in a buoyant element which will multiply his own weak effort and uplift him. Paul would have us feel that as Christians we live and act in such an element. Nothing can be impossible if we have faith in God, who can do all things, and whose power is with us when we do His will. This is the truth which is impressed on us in every chapter of the Epistle to Romans, and we need to realize it in our religion to-day. Relying only on ourselves we have lost that heroic spirit which belongs to the very nature of Christianity.

Again, the faith which Paul insists on is a personal one, your own response as an individual to the call of God. The objection, as we have seen, is often urged against the Epistle that it has fostered a type of religion which centres everything on the saving of one's own soul. Those who so criticize Paul are strangely blind to the fact that he spent his whole life in the endeavour to save other souls. Necessity, he says, was laid upon him to sacrifice all private aims and interests and to work wholly for the good of others. He wrote this Epistle to Romans for the very purpose of making his readers feel that they were debtors to all men, Jews and Greeks and barbarians. Yet he would not wholly have denied the charge that he taught a self-centred religion. He believes that each man has his separate place in the mind of God, and must know God for himself, and make sure of his own salvation. He indeed thinks of all men as bound up together, so that the sin of one involved the sinfulness of all, and by the redemptive act of one the many were set free. None the less he maintains that within the one race of mankind every man stands out by himself. Christ makes His appeal to each one personally, and each one must answer Him with his individual faith. On this conviction Paul grounds his doctrine of liberty. Knowing that in your own person you belong to God and are responsible to Him alone, you must follow the light within you, regardless of the world's judgment, and this liberty which you claim for yourself you must allow to all other men.

In this respect we have been moving away of late years

from Paul's conception of the gospel. He laid all the stress on a personal salvation which is obtained by faith, and we have learned to think of ourselves as members of the human brotherhood. We have grown conscious that no man can be saved by himself. So long as there is evil and misery anywhere in the world around you it will sooner or later recoil on yourself, and you must find your welfare in that of all. This principle holds good in the material life and also in the spiritual. The true way of salvation is to forget yourself altogether and live wholly for your fellow-men. This is the gospel which we would now substitute for that of Paul, and it seems nearer, in many of its aspects, to the teaching of Jesus. But you cannot be of much help to others until you have made sure of yourself. Your work for them has value just in proportion to your own attainment of a new and better life. So long as you are yourself estranged from God you only use unmeaning words when you speak of saving the world.

This is why the Epistle to Romans has a special significance at the present day. We are all full of large enthusiasms. We think in terms of classes and races, and are intent on some novel system which will right all injustices and bring the whole world into brotherhood. It is often claimed that out of this social ferment a new religion is emerging, which is destined some day to take the place of Christianity. One thing, however, is lacking in it, and when all is said it is the essential thing. Religion is personal, and aims at the salvation of men and women. They are not to be saved by some automatic process, when the community has been put right, but it is they who must save the community. Of this fundamental truth Paul is never in doubt. He declares that a man's imperative duty is to see first that he himself is justified by faith in Christ. This conviction of Paul has often been understood selfishly, and has given rise to hard and narrow types of religion which we are now discarding, and it is time that they should go. But the demand that we must look first to our own salvation can never be put aside. We

are personal beings and before all else we are responsible
to God for our own souls. In the Epistle to Romans Paul
insists, with unequalled power, on this primary truth. He
maintains that salvation is by faith, and that faith is the
answer that each man makes for himself to the call of God.
Take this away and you can have no true religion.

Behind everything else in the Epistle there is the assurance
that God has manifested His grace, once for all, in a supreme
act. Paul's message, in the last resort, was the announce-
ment of this act. He admits that men in former times had
arrived at many profound conceptions of God's nature, and
avails himself freely of the prophetic teaching and also of
the wisdom of Greeks and barbarians. When his theology
is analysed it may fairly be argued that he had little to say
which had not, in some fashion, been said before. But one
thing was new and lay at the very centre of all his thinking—
that hopes and surmises had now become reality. God had
entered human history in Christ, and through Him had
effected man's salvation. No idea can be more mistaken
than that Paul was an abstract thinker, who changed the
gospel into a doctrinal system. The very opposite is true.
He has no purpose in his theology but to assert, and if
possible to explain, a concrete historical fact. " When we
were yet without strength in due time Christ died for the
ungodly." "What the Law could not do God has done,
sending his own Son in the likeness of sinful flesh." Our
faith in God is no longer a matter of speculation, of mere
groping in the dark. It can rest itself on something which
actually happened. Through Christ who lived and died on
this earth we can apprehend the invisible God and receive
the gift which He bestowed on men. This was the substance
of all Paul's message. Whatever we make of his arguments,
and he would himself have confessed that they were often
inconclusive, he was only trying to drive home, in every way
he could think of, the marvellous fact that Christ had
appeared and had accomplished the one thing necessary for
our salvation.

The chief value of the Epistle for our day, as for the time in which it was written, is this emphasis on a fact. It is not Paul, but we ourselves who have changed the gospel into something abstract. The whole drift of our modern religious thinking has been towards general principles which we substitute for definite beliefs. Much is made of the historical figure of Jesus, but He is regarded only as a symbol of man's higher aspirations. Sometimes it is maintained that Christian faith would be just the same even though the records of His life were all proved doubtful or though He had never lived at all. The only thing that matters is to believe in goodness, self-sacrifice, the rights of the poor and helpless, the coming time when men will know each other as brothers. This belief, we are told, is Christianity. By long tradition we have come to associate it with the name of Jesus, but it would survive and perhaps would be all the stronger, if it were detached from Him. Our faith must be in the eternal ideas, not in any historical events which may or may not have happened.

At first sight it might appear as if this release of Christianity from mere facts of history implied a great step forward, and as such it has been hailed by many modern teachers. Religion, as we are now trying to understand it, is no longer bound up with anything temporary and accidental. A larger church is in process of formation which will include all men of goodwill, whatever may be their particular creed. Christ Himself will mean far more to us when we honour Him not as an actual Person, but as our highest conception of all truth and goodness. Yet it can hardly be questioned that the weakness of Christianity to-day is chiefly due to the evaporation of its message into a vague idealism. We imagine that faith grows purer when it is separated from earthly reality, but all experience proves that it is only chilled and impoverished. Men are so constituted that they cannot devote themselves to abstractions. It is not merely that they think with their senses and crave for something they can touch and see, but they feel instinctively that what is abstract does not exist. It belongs to some realm of supposition, and has never come into their actual world and has no claim to their allegiance. " My heart," says the psalmist, " cries out for the living God "—for the God who speaks and acts and is real as I am myself. The cry has been repeated by a recent French poet in modern terms: " Blessed be Thou, my God, who hast delivered me from idols, so that I worship Thee only, and not Isis and Osiris, or Justice or Progress, or Truth, or Divinity or Humanity or the Laws of Nature." All imaginary things, whether they are made of wood and stone or of philosophical theory, are nothing but idols. Men can only be satisfied with a reality, which they can apprehend and love.

This is what Paul offers us in the Epistle to Romans. He addresses his letter to the great capital in which all the culture of that ancient world had found its centre, but he does not seek to compete with the high philosophies in which man's wisdom was speaking its latest word. All that he attempts is to proclaim something which God has now done. In Christ He has visited this earth and performed the act which has secured man's salvation. " I am not ashamed," says Paul, " of the gospel of Christ." To the wise it might seem like foolishness, but it has supplied what was lacking in their wisdom. They could only speak out of their own conjecture, but here was a message of what God had actually done, and it was for this that all men were waiting. There can be no religion without faith, and faith reaches out to what cannot be seen or proved. Yet faith must have some assurance on which it can take its stand. If it rests on nothing but a vague assumption it wants that element of confidence which makes it faith. You must lay hold of something which cannot be doubted, and relying on this you are able to venture out into the unknown. Paul finds the basis for his faith in a fact of history. Christ appeared in this world, and through Him God effected the great deed which won us our salvation. Behind the Christian religion there is this certainty.

The Epistle to Romans is thus the grand affirmation that God has acted on behalf of men. Our faith is anchored, not to any guess or speculation, but to something done by God in the sight of all the world. This must always be the strength of Christianity—that it grounds our knowledge of God in a fact. Whatever may be uncertain we can put our trust in God because we know that He once came to us and reconciled us to Himself in Jesus Christ. On this assurance, too, we can build our hopes for the future. The prospect before us is indeed a gloomy one, not merely because our world is lying in ruins, but because we have lost confidence in ourselves. All our projects and endeavours have played us false, and we cannot but feel that they will always do so. But while we despair of ourselves we can believe in what God has done. He has not left us to search in vain for some means of deliverance, for He has Himself delivered us, and requires only that we should accept His gift and put our faith in Him. This is Paul's message in the Epistle to Romans, and it comes back to us with a new meaning at the present day.

INDEX